T0345936

Days Like Smoke

A Minnesota Boyhood

Days Like Smoke

A Minnesota Boyhood

Jon Hassler

Edited and with a Foreword by Will Weaver

AFTON PRESS

Minneapolis - Saint Paul

AFTON PRESS
Minneapolis - Saint Paul

FIRST EDITION SEPTEMBER 2021

Days Like Smoke: A Minnesota Boyhood
Copyright © 2021 by Afton Press. All rights reserved.

Afton Press
6800 France Avenue South, Suite 370
Edina, MN 55435
www.aftonpress.com

Printed in the United States of America
10 9 8 7 6 5 4 3 2 1

ISBN: 978-1-7361021-1-4
LC record available at https://lccn.loc.gov/2021005927

Book and jacket/cover design by Gary Lindberg
All images courtesy of the Jon Hassler Estate

Distributed by the University of Minnesota Press
111 Third Avenue South, Suite 290
Minneapolis, MN 55401-2520
www.upress.umn.edu

TABLE OF CONTENTS

Hear my prayer, o Lord, Harken unto me speedily,
For my days vanish like smoke.

—Psalm 101

Life is perpetually weaving fresh threads which link one individual and one event to another, and these threads are crossed and recrossed, doubled and redoubled, to thicken the web, so that between any slightest point in our past and all the others a rich network of memories gives us an almost infinite variety of communicating paths to choose from.

—Proust

We are children all our lives, obedient to echoes.

—Carol Shields

FOREWORD
BY WILL WEAVER

I'm not fond of long introductions to books, and here I've written one. If you're eager to read Jon Hassler's memoir—a late
and surprise addition to his body of work—please skip ahead.
Who can blame you, and who says you can't read a foreword
afterward? But I hope you'll take a look at how this gem of a
book came to be as well find some fresh insights, perhaps, into
Jon Hassler's writing, his life, and his place in Minnesotan and
American literature.

If you've got the time, let's start, say, in 1993. Not long
after Jon Hassler returned from a private lunch at the White
House with Hillary Clinton, a group of us friends gathered at
his lake cabin in northern Minnesota. A barbecue. A beverage
on the deck. We did not know of his trip to the White House,
nor that Mrs. Clinton was a big fan of Staggerford and other of
his novels—and he did not mention it. This was very "Hassler-
esque," a word I am inventing right here. His personality was
distinguished by extraordinary modesty and humility interwo-

ven with a finely tuned sense of humor. As in, "the joke's both on you and on me." Later he would say of his visits to the White House, "Who would have thought!"—and laugh deeply at the unlikeliness of it all.

Jon Hassler (1933–2008) was born in Minneapolis but spent his formative years in the towns of Staples and Plainview, Minnesota, a combined population of about six thousand. The names of these towns prove that the Gods of Writing have a sense of humor as well. Hassler's novels, including *A Green Journey*, *Simon's Night*, and *Grand Opening*, thrive on the staple rhythms of small town life and the "plain" people who live there. But plain is not to be confused with simple. With his sharp eye for their goings-on, and an unflagging empathy for his characters' travails (often private but sometimes very public), Hassler's novels plumb a richness of humanity bubbling just below the surface of "normal." Alice Munro, in her novel *Lives of Girls and Women*, set in a similar milieu of small-town Ontario, describes "normal" this way: "People's lives in Jubilee… were dull, simple, amazing, and unfathomable—deep caves paved with kitchen linoleum." Substitute the town of Staggerford for Jubliee, and we have the essence—setting and theme—of Hassler's short stories and novels.

Staggerford, for example, follows Miles Pruitt, a thirty-seven-year-old, head-in-the-clouds, bachelor English teacher marooned in a small, northern Minnesota town. In *Staggerford*, as with fictional realism in general and often with first novels, there are well-marked intersections of life and art. I was once in the audience when a fan asked *that* question, the one that nearly always comes up during Q and A: "Mister Hassler, how much of your fiction is based on real-life?" He answered, with a Hassleresque twinkle in his eyes, "Sixty-eight and a half percent." Which might well have been the number! Like Miles Pruitt, Hassler taught high school English early in his career, including six years in Park Rapids, Minnesota, my hometown, where I first came to know him. From Park Rapids, he moved on to Brainerd Lakes Community College and, eventually, as his novels reached a national audience, to Saint John's University in Collegeville, where he was writer-in-residence. Thus in *Staggerford*, Hassler casts a deeply knowing gaze on this outwardly sleepy little town—but one that keeps its eyes peeled when it comes to Miles Pruitt, the unmarried male English teacher in its midst.

In the context of American literature, Miles is a version of Ichabod Crane, the lazy, dilettantish music teacher central to Washington Irving's short story "The Legend of Sleepy Hollow" (1820). Both Miles and Ichabod are artists at heart. Both are odd ducks trapped in a provincial milieu where "real men" do "real work" with horse teams and combines and logging trucks and power tools. Irving's character Brom Bones, the burly farmer who vanquishes Crane, and Hassler's brutish wrestling coach in *Staggerford* are of a piece. If Irving was the first American author to portray New World masculinity as an either-or construct (brains or brawn, a construct that limits us to this day), Hassler's work falls naturally in line. As Miles muses, "In the town of Staggerford, women tended to overestimate teachers' intelligence while the men tended to underestimate their ambition."

Staggerford also dramatizes what must have been Hassler's early artistic stirrings. He had a desire to write, to paint (he was a skilled artist), to do *something* more than carry around a briefcase full of dull, student essays. In a master stroke of artistic control, Hassler endows this most pedestrian of detail—student papers—with symbolism that advances the novel. "I Wish…" is the writing prompt. While most of his students' responses are despairingly small-minded, one or two reach for the stars, thus offering the beleaguered Miles Pruitt and us readers a ray of hope for humankind. The best novels entwine author, characters, and reader in a question of the highest order. Poet Mary Oliver might describe Miles Pruitt's (and Hassler's) dilemmas this way: "Tell me, what is it you plan to do with your one wild and precious life?"

Staggerford also introduces a recurring Hassler theme: a reverence for the underdog, the outsider, the eccentric. Irish critic and short story writer Frank O'Connor called such characters a "submerged population of… the little man [person]." For O'Connor, these included "Gogol's officials, Turgenev's serfs, Maupassant's prostitutes, Chekhov's doctors and teachers, and Sherwood Anderson's provincials, always dreaming of escape." In Hassler's work, they include "the Bone Woman" (*Staggerford*); "the Indian" (*Simon's Night*), a rule-breaking Native American man in an old age home; and "the Grandfather" (*Grand Opening*), a gregarious, fast-driving dreamer modeled after Hassler's own grandfather, Frank "Little" people, marginalized by poverty, eccentricity, mental illness, race, gender or just plain bad luck, capture Hassler's admiration. Their break-outs—occasions when, to everyone's surprise, they rise up against convention and stand tall against insurmountable odds—delight him as a writer. These irruptions nearly always end in defeat, but attention must be paid. Such characters illuminate uncomfortable truths about life and carry value far beyond their lowly status in the town and community. Hassler himself would certainly have said, "At least they tried."

As we consider Jon Hassler's body of work, a logical question follows. Where did his sensibilities—his larger artistic vision—come from? *Days Like Smoke: A Minnesota Boyhood* answers this question. It also lays out Hassler's early path toward becoming one of Minnesota's most popular and best-loved authors. While this memoir will be of great interest to his long-time fans, readers new to his work will be rewarded. *Days Like Smoke* is valuable for its sentences alone, for its rich prose. The memoir is also a love letter to the nature of memory and how it continues to cast light and shadow in our lives. His choice of epigrams to open the book confirms as much: Proust, famous for his deep dives into memory and childhood; and Carol Shields, the Canadian Pulitzer Prize winner, who summarizes Proust's long-winded quote in nine words: "We are children all our lives, obedient to echoes."

Days Like Smoke has an assemblage both simple and wide-reaching. From "Houses" to "Movies" to "Churches" to "Photos" to "Lessons" to "Groceries," he plumbs his memories for what endures—and why. "Bundled in a snowsuit, scarf, and blanket, I'm gliding happily along the icy sidewalk in the box-sled my father has built, and my mother is pulling," though where am I going, he asks? Ah—it comes into focus: they are going to church on a bitterly cold winter day. To the church basement actually—the upper nave is too large to heat in Minnesota winters—where "old ladies pray in the vicinity of votive candles and… the ticking clock measures the tedium." These memories waver into focus as if happening on the page; from them Hassler creates a loop of time, a circle of meaning. "And yet, now sixty winters later, when I go back in memory of Sacred Heart, I go eagerly into the basement."

Faith plays a large role in *Days Like Smoke*. As he wrote in a later, short work, *Why I Am Still A Catholic*, "I was a champion believer in those [childhood] days. I believed every fact, myth, and holy opinion taught me during those first years of parochial school." He was stubbornly a believer—even when a priest once slapped his face for forgetting to say "Father." If his characters, including Miles Pruitt, sometimes call on God mainly to see if anyone is up there—Hello?—it might be argued that the trials of Hassler's fictional characters were his personal method of shoring up his own faith, which seemed never to waver, not even later in life, when Hassler was struck with a terminal and particularly agonizing version of Parkinson's Disease. Andrew Greely, the popular priest, journalist, and novelist, wrote an appreciative eulogy entitled "The Last Catholic Novelist: the grace-filled fiction of Jon Hassler."

If *Days Like Smoke* fills in the role of religion in Hassler's growing-up, it also shows his early fascination with a more secular matter: failure. But failure of a particular kind. He was attracted to characters who were driven by the simple engine of hope, and the more outlandish the hope, the better. Frank, grandfather on Hassler's mother's side, "a jolly, eternal optimist" was fired from his job as a railroad conductor for giving passage to family and friends. Suddenly free to dream big, Grandpa Frank decided to start a laundry in a small town in remote and snowy Saskatchewan. "How he knew this" [the need for a laundry] "was anyone's guess," Hassler remembers, and like all the other of his grandfather's ventures, this one was "a pipedream leading to failure." Hope and failure suffuse Miles Pruitt in *Staggerford*. He is unmarried, stuck in neutral, lost—yet in the end, he dares disturb the small-town universe of racism against Native Americans and the marginalization of the "different." With Hassler-esque understatement, Miles becomes an unlikely hero, though only to those who really knew him.

I first knew Jon Hassler as "Mister Hassler," my sister's high school English teacher. This was in Park Rapids, Minnesota (population 2,900), the town on which *Staggerford*, he has confirmed, is closely modeled. Interested in his students' lives beyond the classroom, he was an occasional drop-by visitor to our farm, which was only three miles as the raven flies from his cabin on Lake Belle Taine near Nevis, Minnesota. He would stop by for sweet corn or tomatoes in season, or sometimes just to hang out and look at things—the black and white Holsteins, the tall silo, the barn, the corn crib, the fields. He was at that time, or perhaps a bit later, beginning to paint landscapes and country scenes. Somewhere there is a small oil painting that features our farm: red barn, white farmhouse, windbreak of pines, green hay fields beyond.

I also remember him as "the guy" who ran the Park Rapids Drive-In movie theater in summertime. My sister Judy, "the popcorn girl," as he laughingly called her, worked at the drive-in, which occupied a sandy field a mile east of town. It was a desolate place in daylight: a towering and slightly tattered movie screen up front; rows of speaker posts—most bent askew from car bumpers; a concrete block projection booth and concession stand in the rear that looked like an ammunition bunker. But by night the little building was brightly lit and hopping, a beacon in the dark, the center of the universe. I often tagged along with my sister for a late evening of B-rated films. Jon manned the ticket booth up front, then eventually came back to the projection booth and concession area to keep an eye on things. He also managed the books—counted the money at night's end—and was last to leave, locking things up and drawing the chain across the entrance at 2:00 a.m. or later.

Days Like Smoke contains a chapter entitled "Movies," and is subtitled *In which the author recalls his movie-going habits from the days when the movements on the screen seemed as personal as his dreams...* Managing The Park Rapids Drive-in was a summer job. Most teachers had one. Still, it is easy to imagine how his summer work at the drive-in might have been particularly useful for a writer (still) in waiting. In my mind's eye, I see Jon in his ticket booth greeting, car by car, everyone in town, or at least it seemed that way to us on Saturday night. I imagine him, now, noting the details of this human parade: their cars, the things people carried on their dashboard, the radio stations, the smells of what they had eaten for supper. He was also onto "all the tricks," my sister confirms, "of kids hiding under blankets in the back seat, or in the trunk to avoid paying for a ticket." But I see him there in his little wooden booth taking money, making change, adding up and salting away, as writers do, the meaning, the truth of this one small town in America.

Being asked to introduce and edit Jon's memoir came with a swirl of emotions. Gratitude. Apprehension. Irony ("Who would have thought?"). Thanks to my own high school English teachers, including Carlton "Ozzie" Anderson, the drive-in theatre projectionist, I eventually came to know Jon, author to author. Early in my literary life, flush with some short story publications, I reached out to the only "real writer" I knew to see if Jon might read my first attempt at a novel. Such presumption! As if he didn't have work of his own! But graciously he agreed, though only if I included a list of questions that I had about my manuscript. I did (a useful exercise in itself). He answered my questions. And I have used this method ever since when accommodating, as best I can, young writers who track me down looking for help. As well, Jon was a loyal friend ongoing. One of my first guest-author appearances was at his invitation to his Midwest Literature class at Saint John's University.

As a newly minted novelist, I rattled on and hardly gave his students a chance to get a word in, as I recall now. But we remained writer-to-writer friends throughout the years, through his books and mine.

At age sixty-four, Jon discovered the answer to some puzzling physical issues. He was the new owner of a debilitating illness called Supranuclear Palsy, a neuromusclar disease akin to Parkinson's Disease but faster moving and also without cure. Life quickly was not easy. But he adapted in Hassler-esque fashion—his Christmas card epistles were works of art. Often they began with something like, "This year I fell down eighty-seven times, which is up from sixty-two last year. But other than that…" His sense of humor, his grace endured.

As will his writing.

Days Like Smoke, at last arriving in print, will only deepen his reputation as one of Minnesota's leading writers, one who could compete with luminaries such as F. Scott Fitzgerald and Sinclair Lewis—but who chose not to. This last point is no small matter. Lewis and Fitzgerald were quite open, especially in their letters, about their desire to "be somebody." Both believed that to reach the highest echelons of American literature, one had to have good novels but also good literary connections; in calculated fashion, both went East to hob-knob with and ingratiate themselves into the center of American publishing. Perhaps to the detriment of his literary career, Jon avoided such self-promotion. He stayed home, remaining loyal to Minnesota as he brought its rich, small-town life to a national audience—and still ended up at the White House. Quite a good joke indeed.

As a posthumous book, the publication of *Days Like Smoke* is a story in itself. His close circle of friends, helpers and typists knew he had been working on a memoir of childhood, but illness complicated all parts of Jon's life. It is easy to surmise that his New York publisher, always looking for the novel, dragged its feet on publishing this "small" memoir. Jon died in 2008. Time and events marched on. *Days Like Smoke* fell through the cracks but luckily into the proverbial drawer where it remained, biding its time until now.

The manuscript came to me via Ian Graham Leask, the passionate publisher of Afton Press, and with the blessing of Jon's family and literary representatives. I read it on the spot. Found it deeply moving, richly rendered, but in small ways unfinished. Most authors would have been quite happy with the manuscript as is. However, knowing Jon and his writing process (revision was key), I was certain he would have gone back through one more time. As I read the manuscript again (and again), I came to see changes he might have made on a last past before publication. Among them, and if revising for today's readers, he likely would have softened a word or a phrase here and there; the term "retard," for example, so easily tossed off by Hassler as a boy and his boyhood pals, carries nowadays an unacceptable sting. Yet, the book was all there. A complete work clearly the effort of months of careful thought and writing. As good or better than anything he had written. *Days Like Smoke* was without doubt the essence of what Jon wanted to say about growing up, and how those early years shaped him. How, unknowingly back then, he was already a "writer in waiting."

As editor, I have made, in consultation with Jon's publisher and family, some changes (the fewest and smallest possible). I think of it as a final buff and polish. I've added a transitional phrase here and there. Fixed a couple of repeated metaphors (perhaps a typist's error?). Turned a couple of richly rendered scenes into sections of their own. Updated a few diction choices.

And reordered a sentence or two for stronger emphasis (for every writer there are sentences that simply defeat us). My largest mark on the manuscript was to move some lovely passages midway in the book to the very end to provide a more poetic and expansive finale. I think Jon would have liked the edits.

CHAPTER 1
HOUSES

*In which the reader is guided from one to another
of the six houses occupied by the author during
his first eighteen years of life and is introduced to
several of the eccentric neighbors who populated
his boyhood, including a happy chicken butcher;
more than one village idiot, as we called them
then; the smartest man in town; and a girl whose
beauty stopped a softball game.*

From the dining room window of the Wilson house at the north edge of town, I could look uphill past the creek to Jonnie Read's house. Jonnie Read was my first friend—a most suitable friend, it seemed to me, for both of us spelled our first names without the unnecessary "h." Jonnie Read's third birthday party was my first social occasion. My eager anticipation turned into anxiety when I discovered his house full of three- and four-year-olds I'd never seen before. From the corners of rooms, I meekly watched them screaming, wrestling, bursting balloons, and gorging themselves with popcorn and cake. Where did all these strangers come from, and why was Jonnie Read paying them more attention than he was paying me? I cried. Mrs. Read called my mother, who came and took me home.

But this party is not my earliest memory. Riding over the snow on a sled was the first event in my life that I remember. My father had equipped the sled with a box to contain me and my blankets, and my mother and I were making our way downtown through a gray afternoon to visit him at work. We passed the houses of Sara, Billy, Frankie, Nancy, and Sammy—children whose existence I was not yet aware of and whose birthday parties I was destined, alas, to attend.

I remember being read to in a rocking chair by my mother's cousin Bunny, who came from Montana to live with us during her high school years. On the coldest days of winter, she sometimes moved the chair onto the register, and we sat in the pillar of heat rising from the coal furnace in the basement. To a boy without siblings, Bunny was a great blessing. I loved the high spirits she shared with my mother. I basked in their laughter.

I remember my first haircut. I vomited down the front of the barber's smock out of fear because, scissors in hand, he came at me all in white, and I thought he was a doctor about to cut me.

When the depression deepened and house rent ($22.50 per month) proved too extravagant for us, we took one of the Nichols Apartments at the center of town. Here we had access to a wide upstairs porch from which we could see the store where my father worked, the church where we went to Mass, the post office

Jon's parents' wedding day

where my mother seemed to derive a lot of pleasure from sending and receiving letters, and the public school where I was compelled to attend kindergarten. Visible from my bedroom was the municipal water tower with its large block lettering—STAPLES—facing east and west. I could see the busy railroad yards and hear the constant chuffing of switch engines, for Staples was a division point of the Northern Pacific. From the kitchen window, I looked down on Bob Batcher's gas station and experienced the first vocational aspiration of my life. I would become a deliverer of fuel oil and drive a blue Pure Oil truck like Bob Batcher's.

In the next apartment lived Mrs. deMars, a kindly widow who smelled of garlic and with whom I sometimes stayed when my parents were away. Downstairs lived the family of a railroader named Elmer Nelson, who hated to be awakened before noon on his days off. When I was five, my parents bought a piano with a view toward making a musician of me. The piano was too large for our rooms, so we kept it in the foyer downstairs. As I was practicing my scales one Sunday morning after early Mass, Elmer Nelson came raging out of his apartment in his underwear and chased me upstairs, calling me a goddam twerp. After that, my parents, ever resourceful, set me to practicing on an improvised keyboard my father made out of a strip of cardboard, with adhesive tape for the white keys, electrician's tape for the black. The fact that I never became a concert pianist, I blame on Elmer Nelson and the discouraging effect of playing scales on that strip of soundless cardboard.

I started kindergarten three days late because I had chickenpox. My mother accompanied me into the public school, the largest building in town, pointed out Jonnie Read and two dozen other small people milling about at the far end of a long room and kissed me good-bye. I was horrified to think of leaving her for the rest of the morning, but I held back my tears and stepped through the door into eighteen years of education. I was halfway down the room when two boys, lying in ambush, came at me with a pair of dime-store hand-cuffs and led me, manacled and terrified, over to a dark closet and closed me inside. I've come to think of that event as emblematic of my schooling. From that point through graduate school, with very few exceptions, I never entered a classroom with anything but the heavy heart of a prisoner, dreading the hour of stultifying tedium that lay ahead.

The day after Hitler invaded Poland, I entered first grade. Sister Simona taught me the Apostle's Creed, Ramona Overby wrote me love notes, and Leonard Nowalski, whenever Sister was out of the room, displayed his penis. In second grade (same room, same teacher), Leonard told me he'd quit smoking. In third grade, under Sister Constance, we went deeper into theology. Why did our guardian angel insist on remaining invisible? In fasting from solid foods, could you have a thin milkshake?

By this time, we'd moved out of the Nichols Apartments and into the Loso house, where we lived from my sixth to my ninth year. (Houses in small towns bear the names of their original or previous owners.) Here again, we had wide and pleasing views from our upstairs windows. From my bedroom, I could see beyond Billy Shelver's house across the alley. I've never been especially aggressive, but once in my life, I've felt the fierce animal pleasure of overpowering someone weaker than myself and giving him a bloody nose. It was Billy Shelver's nose. To the best of my memory, what made Billy culpable was his being a year younger than I and yet having a larger vocabulary. Reenacting Pearl Harbor one day, deploying our toy ships and planes and lead soldiers around a puddle in the alley representing the Pacific

Ocean, Billy had the audacity to utter the word "weapons." It was a word unfamiliar to me, so I beat him up.

Nor had I developed any grace where birthday parties were concerned. I went to Richie Barrett's party with the most wonderful gift I could imagine, a windup motorcycle with a sidecar. I also went with a full bladder. Looking for the bathroom, and too timid to ask, I prowled alone through the Barrett's large house, until halfway upstairs I paused on the landing to water a houseplant, and then hurried home with the motorcycle because I couldn't bear to part with it. The next day my parents made me deliver it to Richie's house, but not before they bought me a duplicate.

A year before we left town, the Scrap Metal Parade of 1942 marked the high point of my student life in Staples. To prove that the war effort transcended religious differences, the public elementary school challenged the parochial school to a competitive collection of scrap metal, which was to be shipped off to factories and transformed into ships, tanks, and ammunition. The competition would end with a grand parade through the center of town, and each school secured a flatbed truck in order to display its scrap along the parade route. My announcement, at home, that the grand marshal would be the student who brought in the heaviest load of metal inspired my father to go down into the basement and size up the enormous cast-iron furnace that had recently been replaced by an oil burner. He borrowed a sledgehammer and spent one entire Sunday afternoon knocking that furnace apart and struggling up the stairs with the heavy parts and out to a borrowed trailer hitched to our little Ford coupe. The outcome was never in doubt. I, a third-grader, was the citywide winner by several hundred pounds, and here in my old family photo album, I see myself posing in our backyard before the parade begins. Grim and apprehensive, like a soldier before battle, I'm wearing a headpiece fashioned by my parents—an aluminum floodlight reflector with a lightbulb sticking up out of its peak and holding before me the American flag on a stick.

In the Loso house I had a dog. His name was Jippie. I didn't often require a confidant, for as an only child, I'd learned the art of conversing with myself, but on those special occasions when I needed to say private things out loud, Jippie was my listener. He was a mixed-blood terrier, white with black spots. He barked only at a certain few people, not everyone, who walked past our house. He took a particular dislike to Mr. Davenport, who used to mutter insults in the dog's direction on his way downtown. Maybe it was Mr. Davenport who fed him ground up glass and brought about his agonizing death in the shade of the lilac bush in our backyard. While my father dug Jippie's grave and buried him, I stayed on the opposite side of the house, playing catch with myself by throwing a tennis ball against the wall. It took him a long time because the earth was dry and hard that summer. I didn't stop playing catch until I heard him put the shovel in the garage and start the car to go to work.

My father's work was that of a grocer managing a store for the Red Owl Company. When I was nine and halfway through the fourth grade, he was promised a new and larger store across the street in a building being put up by a local contractor, but Red Owl reneged at the last minute and allowed his competitor, National Tea, to take it over. Surely my father was vexed, and yet, because it was she who always made our major decisions as a family, I suspect it was my mother's idea to quit Red Owl immediately and relocate to Minneapolis, the city of my birth, where my father found a job in a war plant that manufactured grease guns for military vehicles. We moved in with my mother's parents on South Aldrich, a pretty avenue shaded by a canopy of elms and all but devoid of traffic due to the wartime shortage of tires and gasoline.

Moving to Minneapolis, I don't remember feeling sad to leave behind my several friends in Staples. Indeed, from certain ones of them, I was relieved to get away—Sammy St. Peter, for example, because he was two years my senior, and I, at nine, was a coddled loner easily intimidated by children more mature than myself. Danny's birthday parties, held in the dining room of the Railroad Hotel, were momentous and sophisticated far beyond my years. And Sally Burke, for another example, because by making a close study of her mother, a cynical, prudish gossip, Sally had endowed herself, at eight, with her mother's bitter smirk, humorless laugh, and worst of all, her manner of clinging to me and demanding all my attention. I can't logically blame this girl for what eventually developed into a case of teenage misogyny, and yet it has occurred to me that if Sally had been attractive and high-spirited and possessed of a sense of humor, I might not have gone through such a long dark night of ignorance of all things feminine. How well I remember the relief, in January 1943, of being lifted away from the chubby sourpuss she was becoming.

But there's one in every town. I learned this at Clara Barton School in Minneapolis, where a smug and wily girl named Peggy turned out to be the sort of overweight overachiever Sally had been up north. With this difference, thank God, she displayed no romantic intention toward me or anybody else except our teacher and her idol, Miss Bullard. It's safe to say that I wouldn't remember her across these fifty intervening years if it weren't for her distinctive nickname. Whether this name had been based on an actual embarrassing and witnessed event in her life, or it grew quite naturally out of her family name—Pickering, or Pinkerton or something like that—I know only that all of us fourth-grade boys, those who were near the top in brains and test scores as well as the rest of us who were out of the running, called her by this name with unceasing delight, certain nicknames being simply too inspired and pleasing to the ear not to be repeated over and over, and how beautifully this one rolls off the tongue. Peggy Pickernose.

Although my grandparents' house was scarcely more than a block from the Clara Barton School, none of the boys in my fourth-grade class lived near me. No matter. I was content to while away my afternoons and evenings in solitary pleasures like reading comic books, collecting stamps, and prowling about the house and yard pretending I was a fighter pilot shot down behind enemy lines and sneaking my way back to safety. One very cold day in February, as I tunneled through a hardpacked snowdrift progressing inch by inch across Norway and back to my outfit, I broke through into daylight and found myself being spied upon by a boy I'd seen in the neighborhood but never spoken to. His name was Hughie Lowe. He was twelve, two years older than me. He asked, to my great disappointment, if we could be friends. I sensed what kind of overbearing friend he'd turn out to be; nonetheless, I said okay because to decline would have been impolite, and immediately we took up our roles as lord and servant. To this day, if Hughie remembers me, he probably thinks I liked him, for I was a master of cowardly deceit.

Fourth grade in Minneapolis was Eskimos, long division, and Miss Bullard. Despite Miss Bullard's solicitude, or maybe because of it, I couldn't seem to shake my distress over living in a city where the likes of Hughie was the best and only friend a fellow could find, and where the classroom walls were bereft of the consoling images of the Sacred Heart, the Blessed Virgin, and various other saints and martyrs. I myself played the saint and martyr, putting my unhappiness on display in order to attract Miss Bullard's continued attention.

Let the occasion of Hughie's sawing through my thumb stand for my perfidious behavior as a city boy. Hughie was forever building things out of scrap lumber in his basement. On this Sunday afternoon, we were building bazookas designed after those we'd seen in World War II newsreels. My part was to hold the boards and broomsticks while Hughie sawed. The saw jumped and cut my thumb to the bone. Bleeding and screaming, I ran home, and there I was, duly fussed over and bandaged by my parents and grandparents, and (what a relief!) forbidden to play in Harlow's basement anymore.

Next morning in school Miss Bullard excused me from long division because of my bandaged thumb. As the others worked, she came to my desk and consulted with me in whispers. "And what was it you were building?" she asked.

It took me a while to formulate my answer. I hated to tell her a bazooka. She struck me as too tender-hearted to receive the news that I was manufacturing weapons of war. Surely this would remove me from the role I was playing as her innocent pet.

"A birdhouse?" she prompted.

"Yes, a birdhouse," I lied.

We were in the city less than a full year when my parents decided to buy a grocery store of their own. Consulting with the Red Owl people, they found that the only one they could afford was a squalid little business situated on a short, graveled street called Broadway a hundred miles south of Minneapolis. How such an unpromising store could excite their enthusiasm was a mystery to me, but of course, I said nothing cautionary or discouraging because I was being liberated from the city of my discontent. More than nine months are evidently required for the gestation of a friendship, at least in my case, for when we moved from Minneapolis, I had no one to say good-bye to. I had gone bike riding a few times with a Jim Philips who lived some blocks away, and I had helped a boy named Metcalf find stamps for his album, but there was no one I felt obliged to tell we were leaving, least of all Hughie, the weapons manufacturer.

But Hughie had a sixth sense where I was concerned, and I was making my first trip from the house to the car with an armload of coats and coat hangers when he came hurrying down the street to ask why a cattle truck was backed up to our front door.

"We're moving to Plainview," I told him, bringing happily to mind the village we had recently visited, its water tower, its feed and seed elevator and its two steeples sticking up out of a rolling sea of cornfields, its compact schoolhouse containing all grades, K through 12, and its movie theatre featuring Gene Autry in *Ride Tenderfoot Ride*.

"Never heard of it," said Hughie.

"It's down near Rochester," I told him, pointing to the driver's door of the truck:

JOHNSON TURCKiNG
<u>Plainview Minn</u>
<u>Gr WEiGHT 6 ton</u>

"Rochester! Your car will never make it that far."

"Wanna bet?" I shot back, giving voice for perhaps the first time to the resentment this know-it-all called up in me. This was our new car, a high, square, fifteen-year-old DeSoto that leaked oil and sounded like a tractor. My father had bought it especially for this trip, for sixty-five dollars.

"Cars that old shouldn't be allowed on the highways."

"Who says?"

"My dad." Hughie then stepped over to inspect the truck. Running his hand along one of the slats, he said, "This rig smells like shit."

I pointed out that the two men loading furniture, a Mr. Johnson and a Mr. Brunner from Plainview, had tacked cardboard to the walls and floors so our belongings wouldn't take on the smell of manure. Hughie looked thoughtful for a minute, as though trying to recall a physics formula concerning the impenetrability of cardboard, then he shrugged and went home.

With the cattle truck loaded and its gate securely fastened, Mr. Johnson and Mr. Brunner pulled out, leaving deep creases in the lawn, leaving my mother standing at the curb looking wistful and uncertain, leaving my grandfather full of hearty advice for us, and my grandmother watching teary-eyed as my father climbed into the DeSoto and got its rumbling, popping engine started. I don't recall my mother's giving voice to her misgivings; had she foreseen the intensity of her unhappiness in Plainview, she would certainly have done so. My father, of course, having spent a decade managing a chain store, was eager to take over a business of his own. As for me, I couldn't wait. I was about to crawl onto the pile of coats in the back seat when I heard my name called from afar.

It was Hughie, returning with a going-away gift, a small, framed print I'd seen hanging on his bedroom wall, a Norman Rockwell rendition of a saluting Boy Scout. I didn't want to take it from him. I didn't want to compromise the new and happier days of my fresh start in Plainview by bringing with me any vestiges of my life in the city. Besides, I was ashamed to think, had our roles been reversed, I'd have given Hughie nothing. As he handed me the picture, its hanging wire came loose, and it dropped to the sidewalk. "My stars," said Grandmother, hurrying into the house for a broom to sweep up the glass. Picking up the four dislocated sides of the frame, I said meekly, "Thanks, Hughie," and I crawled into the car and shut the door.

Jon and his mother Ellen at Plainview home

Our first residence in the village of Plainview was the Leahy house at the edge of town, a tall clapboard structure with a cornfield rustling up against the back porch and the stockyards across the street. Miss Leahy herself, a humorless old maid, lived upstairs, while we occupied the ground floor where mice ate the fringes off our rugs. A family of rabbits lived in the basement and ate the squash my parents stored there.

Next door, in a low house beyond a small field of cabbage, lived the Schimmerlings. Besides cabbage, the Schrmmerlings had been raising a flock of chickens, a cageful of pigeons, and two teenage sons named Irvin and Adolf. Mr. Schimmerling, who worked at the feed mill, would gladly spring a nail out of his ear whenever you asked. The younger son, near my age and surely the last American ever to be christened Adolf, asked him to demonstrate for me on their back stoop. "Show Jon the nail trick, Dad." Whereupon, his father put the head end of a large nail into his left ear. We stood close and watched it go half an inch deeper as he pressed on the point, then he lifted away his finger and the nail flew out of his ear and landed in the dirt ten feet away.

Their back stoop was also where Mrs. Schimmerling, a jolly heavy woman, killed chickens. Although I witnessed this butchery more than once, the first time was unequaled for excitement. "Watch, she'll throw the hatchet," Adolf whispered to me as his mother laid the motionless bird on the stoop, her left hand tightly gripping its legs. With an unblinking eye, the chicken watched her raise the hatchet and bring it down—chop!—and then as it began its death spasm, she threw the bird up and away from her, involuntarily throwing the hatchet as well. Lifting herself to her feet and retrieving the hatchet, she turned her back on the headless bird, which went speeding crookedly down the dirt driveway, spurting blood. It tipped over in the tall grass beside the road and fluttered and scratched its way into a small cement culvert and lay still. I was awestruck. Adolf was in stitches. "Don't tell Ma," he whispered.

"Where did it go?" she asked, looking around.

Adolf couldn't contain his delight. He jigged about, doubled over with giggles.

"Now you boys listen here," she said angrily. "A chicken don't disappear into the ground."

I pretended to search among the cabbages.

"Adolf, you seen the chicken go—I'll take the strap to you."

His response was a screech of laughter, so she scurried into the house and came out with a razor strop that dragged on the ground. I watched the struggle from the cabbage patch. She gripped Adolf by the arm and tried to whip him, but he wouldn't stand still. He ran in a circle, turning her around, and the strop, on which she had taken too long a hold, waved in a loop and never caught up with her aim. Instead of increasing her anger, this obviously struck her as humorous, for she began to laugh, and soon they were both laughing so hard they could barely stand.

"Okay," said Adolf breathlessly, pretending to confess. "It went under the house." This settled the matter, for their tiny house was supported at the corners by cement blocks, and the space underneath was too narrow for crawling, the ground too uneven for probing with a stick. Giving up on that roasting hen, Mrs. Schreiber waddled off to the chicken coop for another. Adolf went into the house and came out with an armload of comic books.

On our way to the stockyards to read them, I asked what would happen to the missing chicken. "Won't you tell her where it is?"

"Naw, let the crows and foxes have it—we got lots of chickens. My ma's never any good with the strap. Is yours?"

"We don't have a strap," I told him.

Adolf looked amazed.

The stalls and corrals of the stockyards were empty of stock, as usual. The gates, if you put your weight on the bottom board as you opened them, squealed like pigs. We sat hidden in the cattle chute and rolled big cigarettes made of newspaper and dry alfalfa, and when we touched a match to them, they flared up and proved unsmokable. So we lay back to read about Captain Marvel, Mutt and Jeff, and the Katzenjammer Kids. The wind singing in the knots and cracks of the weathered boards sounded like whining cats.

My first job in connection with the store was delivering circulars door to door. "Find a friend," said my father, "and you can take half the town, and your friend can take the other half." And so, after school on that late September afternoon, we set out from the store with armloads of flyers—

COME TO THE RED OWL GRAND OPENING
LETTUCE 8c a HEAD
BALOGNIA 25c a RING

—and so forth. We left one at the door of every house in town. I was snapped at by a dozen dogs, peered at through glass by at least fifty housewives preparing supper, and frightened by Mrs. Carpenter, the dentist's wife, who came to the door quaking and drooling because she suffered from some fearsome disease of the nerves. (A disease I myself contracted in later years, but thus far without the quaking and drooling, thank God.)

Jon's father in his grocery store

At twilight, turning down our last street of the day, I was warned away from Jesse Patton's house by boys playing in a field across the street. "Don't go in there!" they shouted when they saw me head for the front door of her weathered, crooked house caught in a snarl of dead trees and vines. "That's where Jesse Patton lives. She's a witch!" Glancing through the front window, I saw a chicken looking out at me. I turned and ran to the next house, the skin of my back prickly with fear, and not until I reached the next block was I certain my life had been spared. The friend I chose as my fellow peddler, Dale Montgomery, confirmed the boys' declaration. Jesse was a witch for sure, he said, and chickens did indeed live in her house.

Dale was a fine choice because he knew almost everyone in town. As he worked one side of the street and I worked the other, he called out the names of the people who lived in the houses, and without half trying, I memorized most of those names with the result that by the time we dragged ourselves home after dark,

I knew the names of almost the entire citizenry without knowing what any of them looked like. During the eight years we remained in Plainview, I had the curious experience, time after time, of being introduced to people and seeing, in my mind's eye, their front doors. My parents and friends thought me a wonder, in fact, the way I knew where everyone lived, and although I don't believe I ever gave him credit, it was Dale Montgomery who was responsible for my intimate knowledge of that town, drilling me in that lesson of names in the autumn of 1943 when both of us were ten.

I couldn't get enough of sports. I clearly remember my joy, mid-morning and mid-afternoon in grades five and six, at our being released from the classroom for twenty minutes of fun. I remember how shocked I was during the first of these recesses when Babe Gusa (the most gifted athlete in this class of exceptional athletes) challenged Mrs. Lance, who served as umpire, on the infield fly rule (no one at Sacred Heart had ever heard of such a rule, much less dared contradict Sister Constance), and how astonished I was when she reversed her decision. I clearly recall how my heart fell when I saw Mrs. Lance look at her watch and raise her whistle to her lips to call us back to the tedium of scholarship.

Outside of school hours, my friends and I plunged ourselves into pleasures undreamed of in the city, such as playing football in the knee-deep snow. Such as packing ourselves into the high-decibel, cracker box gymnasiums of the Whitewater League, where we watched the high drama of the Plainview Gophers taking on foes from St. Charles, Wabasha, Eyota, and Pine Island, and knowing each Gopher by name because he was a friend's older brother, or at least the friend of a friend's older brother. Such as, a few years later, bicycling miles beyond the city limits with our fishing poles and pup tents and camping overnight in the bluffs along the Whitewater River.

Jon with his parents

Most of the friends I was making in grade five—Turk, Babe, Kenny, Dale, and Bob—lived near one another on the opposite end of town from the Leahy house, and so it seemed like blessed providence when my parents chose to buy a house in their midst.

This was the Anding house, a bungalow on an elm-shaded lot, ample enough for gardens, picnics, a croquet court, and pickup football games.

Football became my obsession. Basketball and baseball came and went with the seasons, but football we played through the heat of summer and in snowdrifts up to our thighs. When night fell, we devised a game limited to the area of the backyard lit by our patio lamppost, a form of football played entirely on our knees.

Eventually, I came to know the ecstasy of high-school football. Across the street from our house lay the athletic field, newly landscaped and equipped with banks of lights on new steel towers.

"My blood is in the towers," my father was fond of saying, and it was true. In the remarkable effort of community cooperation, the local merchants, my father among them, made monthly trips to Rochester to sell their blood for twenty dollars a pint and thus pay for the lights and towers.

My specialty was tackling. I didn't have much of a throwing arm or enough leg strength to be a runner or enough bulk to play defensive lineman, but I did have the speed and fearlessness of the linebacker. In my maroon-and-gold uniform, number 38, I went up against the ball carriers from Lewiston, Wabasha, Cannon Falls, Lake City, Stewartville, St. Felix, Dodge Center, and our archrival, St. Charles—and I knocked every one of them off his pins. Twenty-seven years later, when the first bound copy of my first novel arrived in the mail, the gratifying thrill was not unprecedented in my life. It was the thrill as great as, but no greater than, the satisfaction I felt in October 1950, the night we beat St. Charles 49–0, on our way to the Whitewater League championship.

"I. E." was the nickname my mother bestowed on the young-ish woman, likely a note or two off mentally, who was placed on the front porch of her small house every day in good weather, there to spend hours writing assiduously in a note-book. Morning after early morning on the way to my summer job at the store, I would see her there, concentrating on the slow movement across the paper, a yellow pencil held in her cramped hand. She was pale and frail and dressed in flimsy lavender smocks with no sleeves. The house itself looked frail and cramped, an old frame duplex standing up to its windows in the weeds of a low-lying lot a block from Broadway. I. E. lived with her mother in the smaller half of the house. The other half was occupied by a pair of elderly women, one an invalid. My mother, walking to the store in the late morning, became so fascinated by the sight of the perpetual writer that one fine day, not seeing her there, she crossed the porch and knocked on the door.

"What!" demanded the girl's mother, opening the door a few inches. A cigarette hung from her lips.

"Your daughter isn't writing today?"

"Oh, yeah? She is too. She's writin' in the kitchen."

"And what does she write, if I may ask?"

"She writes 'I' and she writes 'E,'" said her mother, and closed the door.

My mother had a talent for coming up with the perfect nick-name for anyone a bit peculiar. She gave the name "Rufus" to Clarence Kronebush, a name so perfect (for a reason I don't quite understand) that it carried over into *Grand Opening*, my novel based on my boyhood. In that book Rufus is seen in downtown Plum exactly as he was seen almost every afternoon in our store in Plainview:

In order to go about her shopping unencumbered by Rufus, who couldn't turn a corner without being steered, Mrs. Ottmann quite often led Rufus into Hank's Market and left him in the hands of the Fosters. . . . He was content to stand endlessly at the full-length window of the front door, his hands clasped behind him, his eyes directed vaguely at the people passing in the street, his face locked in its customary grin. When someone entered the store, Rufus shuffled backward and allowed himself to be pressed for a moment between the plate glass in front of him and the glassine doors of the cookie display behind him. Then as the door went shut, he shuffled forward, keeping his nose about six inches from the glass.

Judging by the I.Q. chart we were made to memorize in health class, Clarence weighed in at the lower end of the brain power scale, and yet such was his posture and bearing that if you had seen him from a distance as he walked along Broadway, and if you overlooked his jerky step, you might have mistaken him for a clergyman or an undertaker, particularly in winter when his mother turned him out in his finely-tailored black coat. He was perhaps thirty-five years old. I used to wonder if he ever had anything on his mind, if he understood what he was grinning at, and I decided no, there was no depth to the man at all.

But then one Monday morning, word spread through town that Clarence had another dimension after all, and which I made the subject of a short story called "Rufus at the Door." It was said that during a Sunday picnic in a brother-in-law's farmyard, Clarence had flown into a rage. Scads of Kronebushes attended the picnic, and three or four of his little cousins began to taunt him. They made up a song about his ignorance and sang it to him about two hundred times. He rolled his big round eyes, it was said, and he made a mysterious noise like a groan or a belch—it wasn't reported whether he lost his grin—and he set out after the cousins, brandishing the long knife his mother had brought along for slicing her homemade biscuits.

Hearing about it, I couldn't believe anyone had actually been in danger. I pictured Clarence running awkwardly and too slow to catch up with his quick little cousins; I pictured the knife, a bread slicer, dull at the tip; I pictured his brothers and brothers-in-law, strapping farmers all, who could easily have restrained him. But on the other hand, I could also imagine the alarm. I had attended a few of these farmyard picnics, invited by friends, and I could see how it must have looked to a bystander:

. . . the afternoon lazy and hot; dozens of Ottmanns deployed across the sloping, shady lawn; the children shirtless under their bib overalls; the women at the trestle table, uncovering their tepid hot dishes and runny gelatins; the men smoking under the trees—then suddenly a heightened racket among the children and everyone turning and seeing, to their terror, the youngsters scattering and screaming—half in fright, half in glee—and Rufus hopping jerkily over the grass, the breadknife in his hand, the blade glinting in the sun as he thrust it awkwardly ahead of him, stabbing the air. It was reported that his wild mood passed quickly, and a half-hour later, he and the smaller children, full of sandwiches, lay napping in the shade. But he had given his family a terrible fright. Rufus would have to be put away, his mother was told. He'd have to be taken to the asylum in Faribault.

Never, Mrs. Ottmann insisted. Never as long as she lived would Rufus leave her side. Never before in all his life had he been anything but gentle. How would any of them like it, she wanted to know, if they were attacked by a pack of impudent snips? No, if anybody was coming to take Rufus away, they were coming over her dead body.

This picnic story unsettled us all, and the village at large began to wonder how it would end. Some morons died young, our health teacher told us, and wouldn't it be a blessing if Clarence's mother outlived him. We didn't see how Clarence, after all these years of fixed habits and mother love, could adapt himself to the gruesome life of the asylum, particularly now that he'd exhibited strong emotion. Here then, was a story I was able to finish only when he was Rufus. I had no idea, writing it, what became of Clarence. I was certain that if he survived his mother, he surely must have known unhappiness.

But on a recent visit to Plainview, I inquired about Clarence and learned that fact had been kinder to him than my fiction had been. Mrs. Kronebush had lived so long that by the time of her death, Plainview had a rest home, and there Rufus passed his last days quite peacefully and—who knows—perhaps even happily.

Not all the nicknames in plainview were bestowed by my mother. Loopy was Loopy long before we came to town. Kitty-corner from I. E.'s house stood the filling station owned by Loopy's father and where you might see Loopy himself pumping gas. Loopy had epileptic seizures, and he had them when the chips were down. I must have been fourteen the Sunday afternoon I was sitting in the front row of the new bleachers along the third-base line on the day our town team played its season opener against Hammond or Millville or Conception or another village of the Wabasha County League. In the bottom of the first inning, Loopy came up to bat and had a fit. He dropped to the ground, stiffening, jerking, gurgling, and snapping his teeth. Somebody stuck a first baseman's mitt in his mouth to prevent him from biting his tongue. After he stopped jerking, he was carried over and laid out on the grass in front of the bleachers so his fellow townsmen could keep an eye on him, and the umpire said, "Play ball." I, along with a few others with a low tolerance for the sight of such a pitiful specimen, moved to a higher seat, for Loopy was moaning and whimpering and tears were squeezing out of his tightly closed eyes. Soon, mercifully, he fell asleep. A fan in the bleachers covered him with a blanket, and he slept deeply until the game ended. His teammates roused him and helped him to a car and was delivered home.

Although the war had ended two years earlier, it was Loopy's fondest wish to join the army. He enlisted and got as far as the Federal Building in Minneapolis, where he fell in a fit during his physical exam. Word drifted back to town that his fellow recruits backed away in horror as a doctor knelt beside him, holding a broom handle between his teeth and waiting for his jerking to subside.

How I'd love to put a happy ending on this story—say the federal doctors were aware of a new medicine for epilepsy and Loopy returned to Plainview cured of his harrowing affliction—but of course, no such medicine existed in 1947, and Loopy, waking up on the bus, found himself 4-F and homeward bound.

Jon in the backyard of the Plainview home

Shocked as I was by Loopy's seizure at home plate, I was absolute-ly flummoxed by the sight of the Dickman shut-in. I may have heard rumors about the existence of this nameless offspring of the elderly and aristocratic Dickman family, but rumor was poor preparation for what I saw. This figure, said to be a thirty-year-old female, was kept behind the closed doors of the Dickman's imposing house on the west end of Broadway. Except for Mr. and Mrs. Dickman and their maid, I never met anyone who'd actually seen it, and now that fifty years have passed, I may be the only living soul who laid eyes on the poor thing—an experience I might have been spared if my father, earlier that spring, had not impulsively bought a power lawnmower.

The year 1947 was when Detroit began to catch up with the postwar demand for cars, and we were able to replace our decrepit DeSoto with a gleaming black jewel of a Chrysler New Yorker. (That this was the most expensive car in town, costing over $1,800, was evidence of how far along, in four short years, my parents had brought their grocery business.) Our first trip out of town was a day spent in Minneapolis, naturally, where we paid a call on my grandfather, widowed now and living what seemed to me a sumptuous life, but in reality, was a hand-to-mouth existence at a residential hotel. Later, in Dayton's department store, my father became fascinated with a new-fangled, reel-type, self-propelled lawnmower driven by a gasoline engine. It was a Toro, painted bright green and yellow and about as heavy as an army tank. We returned to the fourth floor twice to look it over and to consider whether our lawn, unquestionably vast, was vast enough to justify the spending of a hundred dollars to keep it cut. I was in favor, of course, for it had been I who struggled to push our conventional mower through the grass every week or two. What clinched it was my promise to cut other people's grass for pay. In fact, I was eager to do so, and I rode home in high excitement, anticipating my first day's work outside the store—evidently feeling the need to begin cutting, besides grass, my Red Owl apron strings.

Word spread quickly—our Toro was the first power mower in town—and soon I had all the lawns I could handle, including the Dickman's, where the dewy shade surrounding their large stone garage, which like so many garages of that era had once been a livery barn, produced a strain of mower-choking grass so tough that I charged them three dollars per cutting, more than anyone else in town.

Ordinarily, I collected my fee from the maid, who seemed to be on duty from dawn till dusk, but there came a time, for some reason, when I went for my pay after dark. I entered a wide, enclosed porch and rang the bell embedded in the heavy front door (you turned a handle, and it rang like a phone), and through the door's oval window of thick, wavy glass I could make out, beyond the foyer, a dim lamp burning on a table beside a sofa. The door was finally opened, slowly, by Mr. Dickman.

Here I must digress to say that Mr. Dickman was one of the most esteemed men in Plainview, but he had grown so old that an entire generation—mine—had no idea why we respected him so much. I suppose our parents could have told us whether he'd been a legislator or a doctor or a county judge, but his past didn't seem to matter. It was enough to think of him as a gaunt old man declining toward death from some great and distant height, never mind what that height had been; we revered him for the decorous manner of his descent.

His hand shook as he groped for a wall switch and turned on a dim light over my head. He said, very decorously, "How do you do." His hair was perfectly white, so was his face, and I saw that he had no idea who I might be or what I might want. I explained.

"Ah," he said, offering me a little smile of welcome, "so you're the new boy in town."

"Not so new," I said. "I've been here four years."

His smile disappeared—either because he disliked being wrong or contradicted. We were still known as the new family in town. He bowed slightly, asking, "Three dollars, is it?" and hobbled off to another room, leaving me defenseless against the creature in the room beyond the foyer. What shocked me first was realizing that the pile of fabric, which I had assumed was a blanket or a sheet, was actually clothing on a human figure— and next, discovering the inhuman aspect of that figure. She appeared to have no shoulders. She lay on her back with no pillow, so that her head was rigidly horizontal, her face turned toward the door, her eyes, pale and lashless, staring into mine. Agatha McGee in *A Green Journey* comes upon this very same sight in the Quimby household:

> Her face seemed not to correspond to God's plan for human faces. Both Mr. and Mrs. Quimby had long faces, but this face was long beyond belief, and since she had a shallow chin and no forehead, most of the length was between the eyes and the mouth.

On her feet were new shoes that must have been sixty years old; the patent leather reflected the light like polished stone, and the archaic ankle straps and buckles were of a fashion never current in this century. Her white dress reached to her shoes, but fit her the way baptismal dresses fit infants, with no conformity to the lines of the body.

Mr. Dickman returned with my pay, his solicitous smile in place once again—solicitude being, I assumed, the natural consequence of carrying his daughter from crib to couch and back again for thirty years—and I hurried away into the night, asking myself the same questions Agatha does:

How could two people's reactions to laying eyes on one another be so one-sided?

Certainly, her presence in the doorway had made no impression whatever on the Quimby girl, while the girl's presence caused in Agatha a bowel-churning shock and a confusing chain of thoughts that would last a lifetime. Why had God given the Quimbys this cross? Could they love this girl the way parents loved normal children?

If Agatha bore a child someday, what were the chances of its being diagnosed, in those old and worst-case clinical terms, as a moron, an idiot, an imbecile? Deprived of understanding and free will, did this girl have a soul?

I hurried home with my faith shaken in the happy promise of life.

Lest I convey the impression that Plainview was populated exclusively with the mentally impaired, I now hasten across the street from the Dickmans and hasten my reader down to the tall house on the corner where Vern Stephens lived. Vern Stephens, everyone agreed, was the smartest man in town. During my eight years living there, I don't believe anyone saw the least bit of evidence of Vern's brilliance, but we had the testimony of his high school teachers—Mrs. Mirise, Miss Miller, and the other old-timers who'd been teaching there for at least twenty years and remembered Vern as a student. They'd never seen such a prodigy, never taught anyone so quick to grasp a concept and remember it. Vern's brilliance broke records, they said.

I cut the Stephens' grass too. Vern was a bachelor, a stout, agreeable man wearing a well-cared-for mustache and living with his sad-looking little mother in the house he'd been born in. I remember two odd things about the house. One, though Vern kept it freshly painted, he always used the same homely mixture—sort of an orangish shade of gray—and, two, its front door was never opened. The doorsill, in fact, stood four feet above the lawn, with no steps leading up to it. To collect for mowing, I went to the back door, which was approached across an open porch supported with spindly pillars, where quite often, I found Mrs. Stover sitting on a spindly chair scowling at the sunset, and more than once caught Vern singing in the kitchen.

Whether the house actually leaned forward, or this was an illusion caused by its sheer face, I can't say. The effect was one of yearning—a house of failed aspirations. A house longing to be on the move. Or was the house imbued with Vern's yearning? What, after all, was Vern doing with his quickness of mind, his photographic memory? He was going to work every day in the canning factory. His job was to operate the hoist that lifted the tubs of cooked vegetables out of the cooling tanks. The vegetables (peas in early summer, corn later) had been cooked in the can, in mammoth tubs, and when they came from the ovens, they were lowered into a channel of cold water and conveyed under the floor of the factory and into the warehouse, and that's where Vern stood with his hoist control in his hand—a multi-button device about the size and shape of a carton of cigarettes. He caused a great iron hook to grip the handle of these rusty tubs weighing half a ton and lift them about four feet above floor level and dump its load onto the unscrambling machine, where another man stood with a short-handled hoe and raked this mass of silvery cans down through a funnel to the conveyor belt, making sure that each can stood on end as it sped off toward the two sharp-eyed old ladies who watched them go by, inspecting them for damage and leaks.

And here, my reader may well ask how I know so much about Vern's position at Lakeside Packing. I know because, during the pea pack of 1951, I was Vern's partner at the unscrambler. I was the man with the hoe. My parents had already moved back north to Staples (my mother, not for the first or last time, trying to recapture an episode of life from her past), while I, newly graduated from high school, loved Plainview too dearly to follow them. And it was while working at the unscrambler during the last day of the pea pack that I caught a glimmer of Vern's brilliance. The entire crew, including Vern I'm sure, was feeling lightheaded at the prospect of a few days of rest before the wagons of corn came rolling in, and Vern, coming at me with a playful look in his eye, recited for me, in its entirety, over the din of the factory and one stanza per tub, *The Rubáiyát of Omar Khayyám*.

Our move to southern Minnesota broke ties, at least temporarily, with my father's family up north. I recall a summer day when I was in high school, however, when a carload of Hasslers arrived for a visit, and it included my cousin Mary, a girl two years older than I and so attractive that her beauty stopped a softball game—and a tournament game at that.

It was dusk. We were sitting on the front porch digesting dinner when the brilliant new lights of the athletic field suddenly came on across the street. My father launched again into the story of his "blood" being in those towers, and soon we saw red caps and blue caps bobbing across the green. (Outfitting a team was a simple matter in that league—only the caps were uniform.) When my father was finally done, I explained to Mary that soon the gridiron would be marked off, goalposts erected, and the Plainview Gophers would take the field. As the starting center and linebacker, I no doubt spoke of myself as an indispensable Gopher, for it's not too much to say that during my high school years, football was my reason for being. But I must have carried on to the point of boredom, for Mary interrupted me to ask if we couldn't go over and watch the baseball game.

Jon Hassler

On our way across the highway and through the freshly graveled parking lot, I explained that this was softball or kitten-ball, as it was then called. Our town team in baseball had already lost its season-ending tournament game, but these guys were still alive, fighting it out with a strong team from Elgin.

Top of the first, Elgin up to bat. There was no grandstand at the softball diamond; fans stood at the waist-high fence running along the baselines. As soon as we stepped out of the shadows into the light, heads began to turn. A new girl in town, a beauty, and escorted by Hassler, of all people. Hassler was anything but a ladies' man. Hassler, who, together with his six or eight chums, paid little attention to girls. Fans moved aside to give us elbow room on the fence. Mary looked over the infielders, and the infielders looked Mary over. The shortstop and the pitcher looked from Mary to each other in disbelief. The shortstop, Bernie Montgomery (the older brother of my friends Bob and Dale), called time out and came over to the fence and asked me who she was.

"My cousin," I told him. I could see the relief in his face; not being my girlfriend, she was fair game.

"Introduce us." Bernie, two or three years out of high school, worked for the editor of the *Plainview News*, learning the newspaper trade.

"Bernie," I said. "Mary."

She gave him a big smile and a little chuckle of pleasure, and I looked at him through her eyes. A fairly good-looking young man, in a blunt-faced, freckly, sandy-haired sort of way, he stood up tight to the fence, his big mitt over his heart, the visor of his blue cap an inch from her forehead.

"How about we go to a movie in Rochester tomorrow night?" he asked her. "I've got a car."

Mary turned to me with a question in her eyes—surely a question, it strikes me now, about his reputation and not, as I thought then, about his car. It was unusual for a man of barely twenty years to own a car in those days.

Seeing the pitcher leave his position and start in our direction, ready to replace Bernie in case he failed, and then seeing the impatient umpire follow him, I gave Mary a nod to confirm that Bernie did indeed own a car, and Mary, applying my nod no doubt to his reputation, gave Bernie another big smile along with her decision, which the hushed spectators were straining to hear.

"Sure," she said.

"Play ball," said the umpire, and the game resumed.

And here, because I based a novel, *Grand Opening*, on my boyhood in Plainview, I must be careful not to confuse my life with my book. "Was there really a Dodger?" I'm often asked by readers haunted by the young outcast who follows the book to its sad conclusion. The answer is no.

But then again, there was Satch.

His name was Jerome, but our fifth-grade teacher, Miss Lance, was the only one who called him that. Satch was a tall, pale lingerer, a smiling, lazy school-skipper, the son of the only divorced woman in this town of 1,500 souls, with a father no longer in evidence. Though he was a couple of years older than me, we were classmates, Satch having failed a good many lessons along the way. He appeared to be totally friendless. I suspect that most parents had warned their sons and daughters away from him—he was known as a thief—so the moment I turned up in town, he was instantly my pal, coveting my toys, my love.

As a newcomer, I was happy enough to have him as a friend, but as soon as I began to be taken up by a better class of friends, I dumped him. For all my instructions to the contrary at home and in church, I must have been a heartless little kid, as demonstrated by how swiftly I closed the front door in their faces the day Satch stood on our porch with a boy he called Duane and asked if they could come in and see my toys. I felt that I had no alternative but to turn them away. For one thing, Duane struck me as vaguely sinister. Obviously older even than Satch and shivering in his coat and allowing his nose to run into his mouth, Duane looked to me like a mobster's goon. Moreover, it was a chilly Saturday morning, and the ill wind blowing straight in our front door was bringing with it a sickening mixture of smells from the stockyards and from the spillage under the oil drums. And to top it off, after school for the past several afternoons I had been welcome to join a crowd of fifth and sixth graders on the athletic field, where we borrowed a football from the high school team, and Babe and Porky chose up sides, and all of us together discovered my talent for tackling. In a brilliant display of athleticism, I impressed even the opposing side by bringing down every ball carrier that came my way. Compared to that, where was the glamour in being a buddy of Satch and his suspicious-looking friend? Satch never played sports. He'd rather smoke.

In view of the week of recesses we'd spent chatting on the schoolyard swings, Satch must have been shocked by my rejection. It was probably my boomerang he wanted to show to Duane. He'd been in our house a time or two and been intrigued by this oversized device of heavy, laminated, and highly polished wood, thick in the middle and tapered at the ends. It really did turn in the air and come back to you if you had enough open land and enough strength of arm to throw it. We had gone out to the field behind the house one time, forty acres of moist, freshly plowed earth, and there Satch, basing his movements on a newsreel he'd once seen about aborigines and their boomerangs, became instantly proficient at throwing it. After turning him away, I hated my boomerang, and never again did I take it out and try to throw it.

I think Satch was with us through that year and part of grade six as well; then he moved away with his mother. I seem to recall his turning up again in junior high, but only for a few weeks. Years passed. Someone reported having seen him in the State Training School for boys in Red Wing, incarcerated for robbery. Decades passed. More recent rumors have placed him in prison, either in Wyoming or Montana.

My suspicions to the contrary that day, his friend Duane was within a year or two of becoming a sensational halfback for the Plainview Gophers. Did I then regret passing up this early chance to befriend him? It's possible—but not for long, because later, during my longstanding crush on my classmate Libby Girard, Duane came home from college one weekend and eloped with her.

Like Frank Healy in my novel *North of Hope*, I too fell in love at first sight.

> Frank was stunned by Libby Girard's beauty. She had large, happy eyes and dark hair. She smiled broadly as she spoke. She had a pretty neck. . . Sylvia Pofford had told him there was a new girl in town and that she was their age but had withheld the fact that she was a knockout.

She was the first of several slim, smart, talkative brunettes who have passed in and out of classrooms I've occupied both as student and teacher, and who, upon leaving, have taken a piece of my heart with them. Let's call her Libby.

And let's call Sylvia Sylvia. You remember Sylvia from your high school days, dear reader; she was the bellwether of your class. She set the standard in scholarship. She was mature, strong of will, strong in her opinions, a wise, unflappable party-giver, unbeautiful, and something of a bore. Libby and Sylvia became instant and inseparable friends.

Libby was so advanced in matters of dating and dancing that I, with no experience, didn't stand a ghost of a chance of becoming her boyfriend, and this may have accounted for a good part of her appeal. An unspoken, unattainable love—love at arms-length—may have been my preference after all. Throughout my life I've had, as I say, a number of such platonic, schoolboy crushes—indeed, they lasted well into my fifties—but none as intense or enduring as my unrequited love for Libby.

> [Frank felt] a kind of liberating relief in realizing that their relationship was not complicated by the threat or promise of romantic intimacy, as though by putting romance aside, they were free to explore whatever else was in their hearts.

Unlike most pretty girls of her age, Libby was perfectly egalitarian in her attentions. You didn't have to be a letterman in sports or outstanding in any way for Libby to take notice of you. In other words, she walked to school with absolutely anybody who came along, and on those mornings when, by careful timing, I turned up on her street just as she was emerging from her neighborhood at the east end of town, she walked to school with me.

Her consistently happy and energetic nature was a wonder, especially when you considered the family she came from. Her father, a barber, and her mother, seldom seen outside her home, wore expressions of such bitter sadness on their faces—as did her older brother—that you had to wonder—and you never found out—if some awful tragedy was weighing on their minds.

We passed a good bit of gossip back and forth during our senior year, for we sat across the aisle from each other at the back of our social studies room. "Jon," whispered late in the year, "I'm quitting school today."

I don't remember what I replied, probably nothing, from shock.

"I'm getting married."

"Duane?" I asked stoically.

The nod she gave me was remarkable for being her last communication with me—unaccompanied by a smile—and I never saw her again.

Sylvia Pofford, while more intelligent, ambitious, and sophisticated than Libby, was less marriageable. She attracted crowds to her parties but not many boys to herself, and when it came time for the senior prom, she was dateless. I was dateless, too, on purpose, but Sylvia's condition was involuntary. In years past, she, like Libby, had cultivated friendships with upperclassmen, and now that we were the oldest class in school, she found that she had cultivated herself out of the running. In the last week before the prom, that week when the would-be promgoer either snares a last-minute date or contemplates suicide, our matching datelessness became a major topic of concern among the mothers of Plainview.

In those days, parents weren't as much in evidence around school as they are now, except when their young entered kindergarten and during the week or so before their graduation from high school. Looking back on my decade of public-school teaching (1955–1965), I see young mothers, every September, hurrying in and out the door at the kindergarten end of the elementary building, and I see middle-aged mothers every spring, passing the door of the classroom where I taught twelfth-grade English, called in to supervise senior banquets, senior field trips, senior awards day, and the punch bowl at the senior prom. The seniors themselves are scarcely aware of all this activity behind the scenes. Emerging from thirteen years in the school system, seniors have grown careless and overconfident, but the mothers understand it to be as tense and crucial a time as kindergarten. For here, too, events could take a nasty turn, and their young could be scarred for life.

So, my mother suggested I take Sylvia to the prom. I laughed the careless, triumphant laugh of the senior about to be released from captivity, by which I meant no, and my mother did not insist. She may have brought it up a second time a day or two later, stressing what a favor I would be doing Catherine, and I was flattered to think that after years of chasing after older adolescents, she might find me a suitable escort, but my answer was the same: "Ha ha," meaning, "No."

Was this my mother's idea entirely, or had the suggestion been put to her by someone else's mother, say Sylvia's? Or, more likely, was it an idea arrived at by any number of mothers who, because their own sons and daughters were successfully paired off, could now pitch in and help the mothers of the dateless? I suspect this to be the case; a match between Sylvia and me was that logical. We had played the two leading roles in the senior class play, our mothers were friends, and until I'd lost interest in grade eight in competing for the best grades, it had been Sylvia against whom I'd competed.

Anyhow, my will proved too strong for the mothers of Plainview. On prom night, I did what I had done every Saturday night for the past eight years. I went to work selling groceries.

Or did I go to the prom? I have these conflicting memories. I recall working in the store, and I remember being in the decorated, softly lit gymnasium when Guy DeLeo, the premier bandleader of southern Minnesota, struck up his eight-piece band. Probably what happened was that Donald Schoewe and I went to the prom for the opening procession, shuffling along at the tail end of it like the unromantic wretches we were, avoiding the eyes of the motherly audience in the bleachers. I don't know what Donald did after the procession ended and we were released. He may have gone home to watch his snowy TV. He may have gone out and got drunk. I know that I went back to the store and candled thirty-dozen eggs brought in by Higgins, the chicken farmer.

I don't think Sylvia was present for the procession. Sylvia, I presume, stayed home and read a book. I would be surprised to learn that she wept or whined or sulked in her room. Sylvia was too strong and smart to be childish about it. I picture her propped up on her bed reading a travelogue about faraway places.

And now I find the grocery store intruding more and more on my consciousness and replacing my memory of houses. I see myself in the Red Owl trimming lettuce, candling eggs, stocking shelves. I see the villagers passing along the checkout counter like the cast of characters they eventually turned out to be in my novel about this village in the corn. I see Mrs. Higgins, for example, asking me "for a pound of Harvest Queen coffee," and I see myself take a bag off the shelf and straighten out the two metal ears that seal it, and I open the hopper at the top of the grinder and flick on the power switch and turn the dial to drip because Mrs. Higgins always takes drip. I tip the pound of beans into the hopper and hold the bag under the chute, and after ten seconds of raucous grinding the blades whine as they run free, and my nose itches with coffee chaff as I switch off the power. It's a minute or more, then, before the coffee smell recedes to the level of the celery smell, potato smell, vinegar smell, Fig Newton smell, sausage smell, and all the rest of the pleasing smells I grew up with.

And here, because of that novel *Grand Opening*, my memories grow unreliable. I can no longer be absolutely certain whether I'm remembering scenes from my life or from my book. In a successful novel, fact and imagination must blend as subtly as the smells in this store of ours. Before the reader opens the book, each of the sixty characters, each of the five thousand images, must be fitted into place, ready to contribute to the pleasing effect of the good read—just as, when you unlock the store in the morning and step inside, the perfect balance of all these innumerable smells indicates that every item is in its place and doing its part to make this a seemly enterprise. Smelling potatoes over everything else means a rotten potato somewhere, and if you're hit with a whiff of vinegar, it means a leaky barrel. It's the perfectly balanced mix that tells you all is well.

CHAPTER 2
MOVIES

In which the author recalls his movie-going habits from the days when the movements on the screen seemed as personal as his dreams; and a chapter ending as it began, in tears, though of a new kind.

Heidi. My mother's sixteen-year-old cousin Bunny, who has come from Helena, Montana, to live with us in our village in northern Minnesota, takes me to the Saturday matinee with her high-school friends. I'm four. It's tragic enough that Shirley Temple should become separated from her kindly grandfather, but when Grandfather looks into a crystal ball and sees her face, I can't stand it. I assume she's trapped inside that globe of glass. I weep, and I wail. Bunny has to leave the movie and walk me the six blocks home, then hurries back to see the ending. To this day—I'm sixty-five—the image still gives me the willies. Bunny, at seventy-seven, clearly remembers her disgust.

Snow White and the Seven Dwarfs. My parents take me to this one. I'm still four. The moment the warty-nosed witch appears on the screen with her poison apple, I begin wailing so loud they have to carry me out and take me home.

Gulliver's Travels. My parents drive me seventeen miles to see this picture at the Cozy Theatre in Wadena. I'm now nearly six. I'm okay until Gulliver is lashed to the ground and walked on by a bunch of creepy little people. I weep. My father takes me to the lobby, tells me to wait there, and returns to his seat. I stand facing the street, now and then gathering enough courage to turn and peek at the screen.

Pinnochio. I'm fine until Pinnochio gets swallowed by the whale; I can't look. I sob and sob. "Scram," says my ordinarily long-suffering father, and I slink out to the lobby. Except for the unwatchable parts, I see the rest of the movie standing in the doorway with the usher.

Dumbo. The Orpheum Theatre, Minneapolis, 1943. Perhaps the first movie I permit myself to enjoy from beginning to end. I see it with my grandfather. The seventy years between us drop away as we respond as one to the pathos and the funny parts, the suspense and the sweetness. For days afterward, Grandfather delights me with his imitation of the tree full of cigar-smoking crows singing "When I See an Elephant Fly."

Leather Burners. Starring Hopalong Cassidy and his two sidekicks, Gabby Hayes and Johnny. Let this movie stand for all the Saturday matinees my friends and I attend between the ages of seven and ten. Jonnie Read, Richie Barrett, and I—and sometimes Sammy Staatz when he feels like associating with his younger inferiors, and sometimes Kenny and Philip Tawney when they can afford it— walk downtown with fifteen cents in our mittens and our holsters and cap guns strapped around our waists. We buy a ticket for ten cents and a sack of popcorn for five and hurry down the sloping aisle to the front row where we join Mr. Tawny, Kenny and Philip's father, an unemployed, emaciated, and perhaps mentally deficient man who takes movies even more seriously than we do. He's often first to see dangers and to shout a warning at the screen—"Watch out, Hoppy, he's behind that rock!"

Precisely at two, when the house darkens and the gauzy curtains part, we turn and shout our pleasure in the direction of the aperture in the back wall over the balcony whence comes the beam of light carrying the newsreel to the screen. Segment one: our troops form a caravan of tanks through a town they've liberated in France; a wrinkled old woman weeps for joy into her tattered shawl; a G. I. smiles down at us from a tank going by and gives us the V-for-Victory sign; Old Glory goes by as well, carried by a color guard wearing dirty and tattered fatigues, and Mr. Tawny stands up and cheers and we follow suit.

In segment two, the same faces turn up each week on battlefields, at the White House, on the high seas, their names forever etched in our memories by the unctuous voice of the narrator: Nimitz, Stettinius, Marshall, Forrestal, Eisenhower; and often the concluding word is FDR's, our great leader urging us on to total victory over the Axis powers. Again, the flag. Again, we cheer.

The newsreel concludes with faraway shots of Dartmouth finishing the season atop the Ivy League by scoring a two-week-old, last-second touchdown against Princeton.

Next, there flashes on the screen, to the loudest cheering yet, a seven-minute *Loony Tunes and Merry Melodies*, featuring Porky Pig and Elmer Fudd. This is followed by a nine-minute short subject, perhaps a *Pete Smith Specialty* (sort of amusing), or a travelogue in dubious color (boo, it's boring) or, if the gods of film are with us, a reel starring our favorite comedy team, *The Three Stooges*, the most sadistic, least funny men alive. Then the serial, in which our hero, Smilin' Jack, foils Fraulein von Teufel, arch-enemy of the free world, and evades what appeared to be certain death in the sawmill last Saturday by regaining consciousness and leaping up from the lumber carriage a split second before the buzz saw can cut him lengthwise in half. In less than eight minutes of carelessly written plot, however, the evil Fraulein is back in control, and today's episode ends with her henchmen dropping our hero, bound and chloroformed, off a cliff overlooking a swamp of hungry alligators. "What happened to Smilin' Jack?" we'll be asked all week by those who aren't in attendance today. "How can he get out of this one?"

"He can't," I'll insist. Never mind the miraculous rescue I watch every Saturday, I half believe Smilin' Jack will turn up dead next week, for I'm the pessimist who never quite trusts the moviemakers to come down on the side of good. I don't foresee the scraggly tree our hero will safely land in halfway down the cliff, nor can I imagine, before I see them on the screen, the tree-dwelling, rope-eating caterpillars that will free his hands and feet. I'm the sucker serials are made for.

And what of Fraulein von Teufel herself? To this day, I can hear the name spoken with hatred and dread, for this serial, like so much entertainment in those years, was conceived as part of what was known as the war effort. I must have taken up the habit of saying her name around home, for I remember my father, a most unwarlike man of German extraction, telling me that I was talking about a devil-woman. How fascinating. To think that people's names could have meaning like ordinary words. Woman of the Devil! To my mind, this was art at its highest form. I was committed to the war effort the way I was committed to preparing for First Communion, that is, with all my heart and soul and by watching "Smilin' Jack," as interpreted by my father, I discovered that the enemy who sought the destruction of my soul was also the enemy of the world at large. And how amazing to realize that while Sister Constance's image of the devil was masculine, Hollywood's was feminine. Sister never said the devil wasn't complex, but to think that humanity was fighting for its earthy and eternal life against some sort of Teutonic hermaphrodite—well, that was almost beyond belief.

And finally, the feature—eighty or ninety minutes of Hopalong and Gabby and Johnny kicking up clouds of desert dust as they lope along through a plot so murky that only Mr. Tawny, our companion in the front row, seems to understand it and only the gunfights draw the rest of us out of a boredom we'll never admit to. There are three such gunfights per movie, so three times, we pull out our capless six-shooters and pretend to fire away at the evil cattle rustlers. During the climactic gunfight, we hold our collective breath as Johnny sustains a serious wound in his shoulder and one of the crooks, the sinister one with the slightly Asian slant to his eyes who goes by Schickelgruber or some such ridiculous Germanic name, sneaks around the edge of the brushy canyon and rises up and is about to drill Hoppy in the back when Mr. Tawney leaps to his feet, pointing and shouting, "Watch out, Hoppy, he's over there behind yuh!" a warning Hoppy doesn't hear but which seems to alert Johnny, who, overcoming the pain of his bullet wound, rolls over and shoots the evil man dead.

Above all other cowboys, Hopalong Cassidy is our favorite. His quiet stoicism and his businesslike devotion to duty give me, personally, the same secure feeling I get when I'm with my father. Moreover, all of us admire him for not singing. Unlike Gene Autry and Roy Rogers, neither Hoppy on horseback nor my father in his grocer's apron would ever think of breaking into song. What can Gene Autry be thinking, wasting entire minutes of our precious Saturday singing stupid songs? Then too, there's Hoppy's tight-lipped manner of addressing women, never allowing them to complicate his life. Roy Rogers, who brings Dale Evans into practically every one of his movies, not only sings duets with her but also gives her an important and tender role to play. I dream of someday meeting Hoppy, perhaps becoming one of his sidekicks. Where would I find him? Where does he go between movies? I imagine him living in a kind of barren hermitage like those in which the desert fathers spent their lives in prayer and self-denial. Roy and Gene would never live in a place like that.

Sergeant York, Immortal Sergeant, Whistling in the Dark, and *Pride of the Yankees.* During our time in Minneapolis, where we have moved for the better part of the year 1943, these are four of the several movies my mother and I travel by streetcar to see while my father worked evenings in a war plant. They reflect my mother's interest in Gary Cooper and William Bendix, mine in Red Skelton.

Apache Trail. My parents, appreciating my love of movies, if not the movie itself, take me on a Friday evening to this dusty western so unmemorable I'm surprised I'm able to recall its title, but remarkable nonetheless for its being my first movie at the Gem Theatre in Plainview, the Minnesota farming village where they have become proprietors of an unpromising little grocery store a block from the showhouse. I'm ten and about to enter grade five.

At the Gem, which stands on Broadway between the newspaper office and Bartz's Bottlegas and Appliance, you buy your ticket from the widowed mother of a soldier killed in the Pacific, and you give it to the proprietor, Mr. Carter, who stands sternly at the inner door and steps aside to allow you into the darkness where the movements on the screen become your substitute for dreams. The violence and sex of this era amount mostly to cowboys shooting horses out from under bandits and Indians, and men kissing women on the lips. The kissing seems quite formal and passionless (the emotion is in the music), and the killing is usually done with small revolvers at a distance of 400 feet.

Mr. Carter displays outside the theatre six or eight black and white stills from the current feature, and I stop there on my way to and from school and reconstruct the plot of a movie I've been to or imagine the plot of a movie I haven't seen and probably won't get to see. So great is my love of movies as a teenager that, given a chance, I would attend every change of program, but my parents, trying to instill in me the principle of moderation, allow me to see fewer than half of the shows that came to town. Babe goes to every show, and so, I believe, does Kenny, but I have to pick and choose.

Rarely, for example, am I allowed to see the midweek film noir feature, and Saturday shows—both matinee and evening—are out of the question because from noon until ten or later every Saturday our store does its heaviest business, and who would pump vinegar and grind coffee and candle eggs if I am at the movies?

Cry of the Werewolf. Inadvertently, my first spook show. Imagine our surprise when, having bought our tickets to see Bing Crosby in *Going My Way*, my mother and I found ourselves sitting in the theatre on the wrong night and watching a normal-looking man enter a small, secret door beside a white brick fireplace and emerge a fanged and savagely murderous animal. This was the year I turned twelve and began staying home alone when my parents went out in the evening, and it was also the year—by a horrifying coincidence—that my father painted our brick fireplace white. Alone in the house after dark, I tried staying in my room with the door shut, but of course, every creak of the wind indicated the fireplace door was opening, and I was trapped in my bedroom. So, I ventured out to the living room and bundled myself up on the couch, where I fell asleep watching for the creature with the killer fangs. It was another year or more before the effect of that movie wore off, and I dared, when home alone, to go to bed.

Kiss of Death. My favorite film noir of the 40s due to Richard Widmark's stupendous portrayal of Tommy Udo, the clean-cut psychotic killer with the frightening sneer and the crazy giggle. This role, Widmark's first, earned him his only Oscar nomination. So strong is his performance that he seems to have carried the rest of the cast with him, both Victor Mature and Brian Donleavy rising to unprecedented heights of believability.

What drew me to Tomy Udo?—me, perhaps the only school-boy of his generation not to have been involved in a schoolyard brawl, whose one and only experience with fisticuffs had been punching, at the age of seven, Billy Shelver in the nose because he knew more words than I. It's my guess that my sixteen-year-old psyche was opening a window on the dark side of my nature and quickly closing it again. Surely, this need now and then to indulge my wicked urges accounts for the unceasing delight I still take in the diaries and letters attesting to the meanness of Evelyn Waugh. I have yet to meet anyone who enjoys Waugh's banana story as much as I:

Toward the end of World War II, the British government, as a morale booster, imported a shipload of bananas and gave them to households with children, many of whom, because of the privations of war, had never seen a banana. As soon as his were delivered, Waugh summoned his children to the dining room for instruction, and there, with the three of them sitting obediently at table watching, he proceeded to slice the bananas into a single bowl, pour milk and sugar over them, and eat them all himself.

Okay, dear reader, here's a milder one, if only because his victim this time was not so innocent as his children. I dare you not to savor this remark about his sometime friend, enemy, and drinking companion Randolph Churchill, about whom, (after Randolph had undergone surgery for a tumor that proved to be benign) Waugh remarked in a letter, "How typical of the medical profession that they should find the only part of Randolph that's not malignant and remove it."

Such were the movies of my boyhood, all of which transported me impossibly far from Plainview, Minnesota. But one weekend a remarkable thing happened at the Gem: most of Plainview sees Kenny's brother in a newsreel. Kenny's brother is a student at the US Naval Academy, and on this particular Friday evening, my friend Turk, sitting beside me, suddenly points at the screen and exclaims, "Hey, there's Kenny's brother." Having never met the young man, I, of course, am not able to pick him out of the sea of midshipmen cheering for their team in a losing cause against Army's invincible backfield of Mr. Inside Blanchard and Mr. Outside Davis, but Turk is certain. He goes to the lobby and phones Kenny, who comes to the second show and confirms the sighting. Word spreads, and the next day at all three shows—two o'clock, seven, and nine—every seat is filled. Until this odd occurrence, I have seldom heard the young man's name mentioned, but for the rest of his time at the Academy, Kenny's brother is the talk of the town. It's as though, until now, his naval career had been too vague to be imagined, but his image on the screen made it real.

This sort of validation by film, as I call it, has come to haunt me as a novelist. "Any of your books been made into movies?" is the universal question I'm asked on the speaking circuit, and it isn't only film students and couch potatoes doing the asking. It's serious readers whose judgment I respect. It's chairmen of English departments; it's my cousins, my friends. And the breath-holding manner with which my audience awaits the answer tells me that this is the most crucial inquiry of the evening, that seeing a movie based on a book validates the book, that only through the movie can they fully understand and enjoy the book.

And, although it seems like a case of mixed-up priorities, I can't say I blame them. Movies are that powerful. I never laugh out loud or cry real tears when reading a book, but lately, I've been doing both at the movies. I must be developing, in my old age, a strong sentimental streak because the happier the ending, the wetter my cheeks when I emerge from the darkness. *The Joy Luck Club* was the first movie where, as a grown man, I lost control. Watching *Brassed Off* recently, I foresaw the happy ending practically from the beginning, and so I wept throughout. It has to do with great odds overcome. A reconciliation after two hours of struggle trips a switch in my heart. I want to stand up and shout at those around me, "What is more beautiful than this!" But, of course, I don't. I sit there, sobbing as though I were four.

CHAPTER 3
CHURCHES

*In which the author remembers the sisters, clergy, and
friends who contributed to his religious upbringing,
including an eight-year-old terrorist, a twelve-year-old
saint, and concludes with an explanation of why he
chooses to remain a churchgoing Catholic.*

Bundled in a snowsuit, scarf, and blanket, I'm gliding happily
along the icy sidewalk in the box-sled my father has built, and
my mother is pulling. It doesn't occur to me that this daily trip
downtown in all weather is a measure of my parents' devotion
to one another; I'm only four and too self-involved to understand any but their equally strong devotion to me. I have begun
to sense, however, that my father has a competitor—somebody
named God—for my mother's attention, because whenever it's
below zero, and the north wind bites at her exposed calves (this
is about five years before the first respectable woman in Staples
will wear slacks in public), it's always at Sacred Heart Church
where we stop for a few minutes' shelter. But not in the church
proper. This is the Depression, and the cost of heating the vast

reaches of the upper church through a Minnesota winter is more than this congregation can afford. We enter the vestibule and descend into the whitewashed, low-ceilinged basement, where Father Donnay has fashioned an altar and brought in a variety of cast-off kneelers and pews and slatted folding chairs that creak when you squirm, and it's here my mother takes out her rosary and gives herself up to her Maker. She talks with Him, she says. So does old Mrs. Crouch apparently, whom we inevitably find kneeling at the communion rail with her alarm clock ticking loudly at her elbow and her tall son sitting behind her in the front pew looking alert and weirdly happy.

These visits don't do much for my relationship with God. I don't like it down here. It's not Sonny Crouch who repels me; I can tell by his constant smile that he's harmless. Nor is it particularly gloomy in the basement; the ground-level windows are large enough to catch a good bit of the southwest-sinking sun and bounce its pink light off the far wall where a couple of other old ladies are praying in the vicinity of the votive candles. It's the ticking clock I dislike, and the tedium it measures out. It's terribly dull down here. I've had my nap, and I want to be on my way. I've long since given up trying to have a conversation with God. I used to listen, but he never said anything.

I'm eager to get to the grocery store and see my father in his apron. I'm hungry for the piece of candy he'll give me.

After what seems an eternity, we're suddenly stirred to life by the shrill alarm of Mrs. Crouch's clock. It's ten minutes before *Jack Armstrong*, which she claims is Sonny's favorite radio show. Mother knots my scarf tightly under my chin, and Mrs. Crouch zips up Sonny's jacket. The other two old ladies grunt and sigh, rising arthritically to their feet. These are the Macklin sisters-in-law who come every day to pray for the repose of the soul of their brother and husband, who died, says my mother, in a farm accident. That these two women resemble each other greatly amuses my mother. The Macklins were married so long, says Mother, that Mrs. Macklin came to resemble not only her husband but also his sister. Outside, Mother joins the three other women in a brief knot of gossip under the smiling gaze of Sonny Crouch. I can't stand to wait another minute. I break free and run to my sled.

And yet now, sixty winters later, when I go back in memory to Sacred Heart, I go eagerly into the basement. It's only with effort that I picture Father Donnay and his acolytes in the upper church—at Easter, say, engulfed by the lilies festooning the raised sanctuary with its hand-carved high alter imported from France. Upstairs there's too much color and space to take in, too much mystery to puzzle over, too many people crowded into the waxed and polished pews. All but faded from memory are the gigantic and resplendent saints in the window glass and the sculpted saints looking patiently down from their niches over the side altars. Pardon me while I slip down into the basement where my initial, ascetic impression of Catholicism was formed, down under that low ceiling where the Crouches, the Macklins, my mother and I watched the dying daylight play over the whitewashed walls as we listened for God in the tick of the clock.

The nuns of Sacred Heart School were my teachers in the primary grades. In first grade, Sister Simona taught us the Apostles Creed, Ramona Overby wrote me love notes, and Leo Kranski, whenever Sister was out of the room, displayed his penis. In the second grade (same room, same sister), Ricky

Burke told me he'd quit smoking; Father Donnay, on his name's day (December 6, the Feast of St. Nicholas), presented each of us with a small red apple; and I, on December 7 or 8, beat up Billy Shelver. I was both thrilled and terrified by the sight of his blood and tears, but my memory of this event will forever be tied up with my memory of Father Donnay's apple, a frightening experience unmitigated by any sort of thrill. I carried the apple home from school and forgot it until, weeks later, I found this sacred gift turning black with rot at the back of the refrigerator. Here was a sacrilege too serious to be forgiven, and I lived for weeks with the dread of the hellfire awaiting me when I died. I might have sought consolation from my confessor if he weren't the same man who'd given out the apples.

In third grade, under Sister Constance, we went deeper into theology. Why did our guardian angels insist on remaining invisible? In fasting from solid food during Ember Days, could we have a thin milkshake? Was I guilty of a serious sin when, standing in line at the confessional, I overheard Ricky Burke confess that he fought with his brothers? Sister was stumped by the first question, declared no to the second, and found both Ricky and me guilty in regard to the third.

I was a champion believer in those days. I believed every fact, myth, and holy opinion taught me during those first years of parochial school. I believed in the Communion of Saints, the Knights of Columbus, the multiplication tables, and life everlasting. I believed in the efficacy of prayer, fasting, phonics, scrap metal drives, and war bonds. The one thing I had trouble believing was Sister Constance's prohibition of the word "leg." She said we must always say "limb" because "leg" had improper connotations. I never believed that.

Our house on South Aldrich in Minneapolis stood a dozen long blocks from the Church of the Incarnation, a handsome Romanesque structure with white marble statuary standing out against the dark brick, but without (it seemed) a basement. Here, in 1930, my parents had been married, and here, on Easter Sunday 1933, I had been baptized.

Surely our household of five went to Mass every Sunday (a serious strain of religious devotion came down to me out of Bavaria on my father's side of the family, out of Ireland on my mother's side), and yet I don't recall a single Mass at Incarnation. What I do remember are the rather sparsely attended Tuesday evening devotions my mother and I walked to throughout the spring and summer of 1943 (my father, on night shift, went to work at suppertime), and how earnestly we prayed for victory followed by world peace. I remember the coolness of the vast empty spaces between the faithful during May and June, and then, during August, the heat trapped inside as the days shortened and cooled. This was the year I came to love, under my mother's guidance, singing "Tantum Ergo" and lighting votive candles. This was also the year, I believe, that my sainted grandmother, in that very church, was refused absolution and cast out of the confessional by a roaring priest whose name we never learned and whose form of insanity we speculated about for years after we left the city.

Which we did, eventually, moving to Plainview, where I, at the end of our first week in town, conspired to derail a train—a thrilling and terrifying experience. That the instigator, Timmy Musser, was only eight years old and probably not of sound mind was immaterial to me. While my parents and the nuns of Sacred Heart had trained me in the art of willing obedience, they hadn't gotten around to discernment, so I had no mind of my own. Whenever I was allowed to attend one of the mobster movies of that era, I seldom identified with either the chief detective or the gang leader but recognized myself in the role of some stupidly obedient henchman.

The Mussers, a Greek- or Latin-looking family of four, lived across the street from the high, drafty house we shared with the Widow Leahy. Their house sat very low, as though in a ditch, their front threshold well below street level, their back door pushed up to the enormous oil tanks beside the railroad embankment. They were given to odd behavior. Mrs. Musser, for example, preserved meat the way I had seen my mother put up peaches and tomatoes—in jars to store in the cellar. Furthermore, she left the confines of her house and yard only once a week, at six am on Sunday morning, to attend Mass. Mr. Musser, unlike my own father, never lifted a finger to help around the house. Evenings he divested himself of his work clothes down to his socks, pants, and suspenders and took his ease on the couch, ignoring the loose door hinges and cracked windowpanes while he droned on about his job at the nearby Lakeside Packing Company. His wife, busily darning socks or knitting, appeared to be listening to him, but no one else did. Not I, who lay on the floor with Timmy, trying to teach him the game of checkers; not Timmy, whose conniving, criminal mind had no room in it for games or make-believe or whimsey of any sort; nor Lou, his older sister, a Latin beauty who busied herself with her high school homework under the dim and only lamp in the room. Lou's odd behavior was tied up with her holiness. She never went out with boys or read magazines, her mother told me proudly, and she saw only religious movies such as *Song of Bernadette*. What's more, she went to confession every week.

Lou was preparing herself to follow in the footsteps of an older sister and become (in Timmy's words) "a goddam nun out in California." God had called her, said her mother.

If God was leading Lou into the convent, then Satan must have had prison in mind for her brother. Already as a third-grader, Timmy Musser had the instincts of a hardened gangster. He wore on his little round face an unchanging expression of great seriousness, and by the unceasing movement of his eyes, deliberate rather than shifty, he seemed always to be planning his next heist while checking to see if he was being followed.

The day we tried to derail the train began with Timmy opening the front door of our house and calling, "C'm on, we gotta go listen to Axel Johnson swear!"—an invitation I wouldn't have been permitted to accept, had my parents heard it, but they had left for the store early in the morning, leaving me in the negligent hands of Miss Leahey, the spinster upstairs.

I hurried across the street in the lovely September sunshine and followed Timmy into the stockyards, where Mr. Johnson was backing his truck up to the cattle chute. We sat side by side on the top rail of the fence surrounding the central corral and concentrated on the spectacular curses falling from the lips of the trucker as he drove a squealing mass of pigs down the chute to wait for rail transportation to the next stage of their short, unhappy lives. "Goddam, you asshole swine!" Johnson shouted angrily from the shadowy interior of the very truck that had brought our furniture to town. "Git your shitty assholes down the goddam chute!" Whipping and poking the bewildered creatures with a sharp stick, Johnson caused them to panic and form tight knots in the narrow chute, which angered him all the more. He raged, jabbing them with insane fury. Never again in my sixty-odd years of life was I to witness such a rich and comprehensive and brutal performance of this kind. Only a few of the words were new to me, for Timmy had been briefing me on definitions, concentrating on the various forms of the f-word, but it was nonetheless shocking to hear this language put to such intense and furious use.

By the time Johnson followed the last poor pig out of the truck, his face was scarlet and running with sweat. From a thermos in the cab, he poured himself a tin cup of coffee, drew a sandwich out of a sack, and leaned on the fence to eat and watch the snorting animals scurry across the sun-drenched corral looking for shade.

"Hey August," shouted Timmy, "How many them fuckers you bring in, all told?"

Johnson ignored this inquiry. He was busy kicking pigs away from the narrow strip of shade at his feet.

"C'm on," said Timmy, jumping down from the fence, and I respectfully followed him around to the passenger side of the cab and the toolbox bolted to the running board. Carefully and silently, he lifted out an enormous crowbar and tossed it into the weeds. "We'll need that to tip over the train this afternoon," he said.

This was the same train that chugged sporadically into the village of Plum in my novel *Grand Opening*, a train of two or three cars that crossed the prairie, sometimes backward, caboose first, on a meandering track from the direction of Rochester. Early September being the culmination of the corn pack, the train was showing up five and six days a week.

By the time it arrived in mid-afternoon, frontwards, we were hidden among the gigantic fuel oil drums behind Timmy's house. We watched its engine and coal tender uncouple itself and back onto the spur behind the factory warehouse, hook up the waiting ox car and then reattach itself to the rest of the train. It stopped next at the stockyards where it took Mr. Johnson and Mr. Brunner a full half-hour to get the elusive pigs up a chute into the cattle car. Timmy was tense, waiting to see if it would come further into town or go back where it came from. It chugged past us and rounded a curve to the grain elevator at the center of town, and as soon as it was out of sight, we scampered down to ground level, and I watched for traffic at the crossing while Timmy inserted the crowbar in a switch. He'd tried this twice before, he told me; the first time he'd put a board in the switch well before the train arrived, but it came to town frontwards, and the engineer saw it and stopped, and a fireman had descended from the locomotive and kicked it away, assuming (Timmy thought) that it was construction debris. The second time he'd planted an oak two-by-six in the switch after the train had gone further into town and nearly succeeded. The caboose had rocked but stayed upright, and the crew hadn't noticed because the brakeman had left his place in the caboose and was riding with the other two crew members in the locomotive.

Then we scrambled back up to our perch. This being the highest point of land for miles around, I found that I could see clear across town to the athletic field where a bunch of kids who appeared to be about my size were playing football. I could see the bell towers of the two biggest churches in town, St. Joachim's Catholic and Immanuel Lutheran, standing as sentinels of the soul at opposite ends of Main Street. I could see the roof of the Red Owl and wished I were there instead of shivering in the damp wind at the top of this rusty oil drum waiting to see a disaster I'd helped to bring about.

Timmy, suddenly alert to the distant ding-dong of the bell and the chuffing of steam, said, "Damn to hell," and pointed down at the switch. The crowbar, worn shiny from use as a tire iron, was glistening brightly in the sun. "They'll see it, dammit, they'll see it."

"No, they won't," I said, hoping they would. Now, with the train backing lazily around the bend, I was terrified. Someone would die. We would be caught and put in prison.

On chugged the train, neither slowing down nor speeding up. "Damn them fartblossoms," seethed Timmy, "they ain't going fast enough to tip over." With my heart in my throat, I watched the caboose hit the switch and teeter. Fearful as I was, I felt triumphant as well, inasmuch as the scene below me proved that one could work one's will on the world. It only required that you were calculating enough beforehand and sneaky enough to carry it out. Choosing a weaker victim was essential, of course, the way I had chosen Billy Shelver to administer a bloody nose to, the way this third-grade prodigy at my side had chosen a mere railroad train and its crew.

The caboose didn't tip over or slip off the rails. It stopped, still rocking, and the brakeman stepped out on the back platform and looked every direction but up. The engineer and fireman came running.

"We better go," I said, shrinking back from the edge of the oil drum we lay upon.

Without taking his eyes from the tracks, Timmy asked why.

"We'll get caught," said I, finding with my foot the top rung of the ladder.

I understood why Timmy wanted to stay—what was the good of an act of violence if you weren't around to study the consequences?—but I'll never understand where he got the courage to do so, to keep poking his head over the edge to take it all in, right up to the point when the crew climbed aboard and the rest of the train drew slowly across the switch and then, with a triumphant toot and ding-dong, chugged off between the fields of corn. I wasn't there for that part. I was listening from the safety of the Mussers' kitchen where, dripping the sweat of fear and panting with relief, I was watching Timmy's beautiful and saintly sister help the reclusive Mrs. Musser stuff handfuls of cooked beef into glass jars.

Within a month of our arrival in town and completely untutored, I began to serve Mass at St. Joachim's. This being a nunless parish and its old and ascetic pastor, Father O'Connor, being too far removed from the mundane to bother instructing a mere child of ten, I apprenticed myself to the only experienced server in the parish, a boy named Jackie.

Jackie was the good-natured youngest child of a widow who cleaned houses for the two or three well-to-do families in town. He was two years older than I, and the object of my great admiration, not only because he was a faultless altar boy—dedicated, devout, punctual, and obedient—but also because he seemed smarter than a lot of Catholics I knew, and he had a wry sense of humor. (At this point in my life, it seemed to me that I had met, among the truly religious, an overabundance of humorless types, and I'd begun to suspect that slowness of mind might be a prerequisite to holiness.) Whenever Fr. O'Connor lost his way in the pulpit and followed an irrelevant path into private musings, Jackie would turn his wise little grin in my direction as if to say, "How pathetic" and hope, I'm sure, for an answering grin from me.

Outside of church, however, we saw very little of one another—such is the age gap between a fifth-grader and a seventh-grader—and yet, when at the end of our first year in town, we left the Widow Leahy and the stockyards and moved to what I've come to think of as the ideal house at the opposite end of an ideal town, I found myself living just a few doors down the block from Jackie. I imagined that somehow, despite the difference in our ages, we might become chums, but it was too late for that. By this time, Jackie was dying.

I was perhaps his only regular visitor. I went every Saturday after lunch. His mother had converted the front room of their small house into Jackie's bedroom, where he could watch the passing traffic on Highway 42 from his bed. What did we do or say during my visits? We may have played a hand or two of rummy, and maybe we looked over the assignments I brought him from his homeroom teacher, but I have no memory of anything but inconsequential small talk. It's a characteristic of anyone growing up in a happy household, I've found, this ability to wring every possible remark out of an unremarkable topic. Around people we're fond of, our urge to converse is far greater than our need to do so, and we, therefore, talk at length about little, stringing out our words the way spiders emit the filament of their webs. In the grocery store, imitating my parents, I was growing proficient at small talk, particularly with old people, and Jackie was about as old as he was going to get.

At first, I went to see him under orders from my mother. Visiting the sick was a corporal work of mercy after all, and she was eager for me to start building up some credit in eternity— and at no risk, for rheumatic fever, unlike polio, was said to be noncontagious. But I soon found myself making these weekly visits of my own accord, for I was finding more and more about Jackie to be fond of, and curious about.

"This seeing the sick endears them to us," says Gerard Manley Hopkins, which of course, is true, but as compelling as my fellow-feeling was my curiosity about the physical changes worked upon him by his weakening heart. He was going through the same shrinking stages we witness now and then in a public figure who will allow himself to waste away on the television news—recently Cardinal Joseph Bernardine of Chicago, Vice President Hubert Humphrey twenty years ago—but I'm not talking about this physical transformation so much as a change from within. His illness seemed to relax him, seemed to purify him, seemed to lend him a kind of transparency through which I could see quite plainly the sweetness of his soul.

One sunny day in late autumn, for example, gazing out the window, Jackie's eyes settled on the distant athletic field, and he remarked, "I can see you guys playing football over there after school." He said this without a trace of envy in his voice, no hint of anguish or despair. Whereas I, with my obsessive love of football, would doubtless have been bitterly frustrated in his place, Jackie seemed to be speaking out of sheer pleasure.

Or again: one of his older sister's husbands, dismayed by Jackie's loss of weight, stopped by with a quart of ice cream one Saturday and demanded that he eat all of it nonstop. This was shortly before my arrival, and I found Jackie looking bloated and amused as he slowly spooned up the last of the ice cream. His brother-in-law stood over him, looking smugly full of himself, believing, I suppose, that he'd just discovered the cure for rheumatic fever. And Jackie's sublime smile said that he believed it too, but of course, this was for his brother-in-law's benefit only, for when he turned to look at me, I saw a flicker of the old wryness in his eyes. "We'll get some meat on that kid's bones yet," the brother-in-law explained to me on his way out. "I'm coming back tomorrow with another quart." With his savior safely out of the way, Jackie asked me to bring him the basin from the drainboard in the kitchen; then he asked me to please go outside and come back later. Leaving, I heard him begin to vomit.

God knows how many quarts of ice cream Jackie put down and later brought up in order to sustain his brother-in-law's hope. I only know that the more I saw of Jackie's self-abnegation, the more fascinating it became. Wasn't this the same sort of God-pleasing humility the Church of Rome had been urging on me since the first grade? But with this difference: Jackie wasn't being humble for God's sake, or the Church's, or even his brother-in-law's; he was simply being himself.

Here, then, was virtue in its pure form, and I found it every bit as attractive as Timmy Musser's evil bent. I longed to be as good as Jackie, and yet, at the tender age of eleven and twelve, I somehow knew that to reach Jackie's level of virtue, I would need to drop my pride, my self-regard, the very idea that I was being virtuous. I was much too self-aware to be as good as Jackie.

Or as bad as Timmy, for that matter. For isn't it this same lack of self-regard that allows the thief, the terrorist, the train de-railer to carry out his mischief? So, I would never be a candidate for either sainthood or prison. With my proclivity for patient watchfulness, I would always play the role of the idle bystander. I could thrill to tales of derring-do, and I could admire sainthood, but I'd never come close to either end of the morality scale. My place was at the intersection, watching for traffic while the crowbar is inserted in the switch. My place was in the chair beside the deathbed.

I made one last trip to his house, this time in the evening, with my parents, to view his body. We found the kitchen crowded with Jackie's brothers (one wearing a Navy uniform) and mother and sisters and their families. Jackie, in his coffin, had the front room practically to himself while we the living ate his mother's homemade cookies and made cheery small talk. We were reluctant to leave each other's company for more than the few seconds it took to step through the open doorway and mumble a prayer over the body. I didn't even do that. I, who had given him a part of every Saturday for almost a year, had no time for him now.

It was a dark rainy morning when most of the eighth grade and I from the sixth were released from class and hurried down the street to St. Joachim's, where I put on my black requiem cassock and my white surplice, and then, bearing the crucifix on a staff, I led Father O'Connor down the middle aisle to meet the coffin and the drenched mourners in the vestibule. After a brief prayer and a sprinkling of holy water, I turned around and led the procession into the crowded church as the organ and choir broke out in their loud lament, which was made even graver than usual, more sorrowful, by the undertone of the rain pounding relentlessly on the roof.

And yet, I didn't feel the sting of Jackie's death during his funeral. I was too full of myself as an altar boy, imagining how I must look to my schoolmates, particularly the Protestants and the nonchurchgoers. How admirably I went about my duties on the altar. How amazing and mysterious were the phrases I cried out in sharp contrast to Father O'Connor's mumbled prayers. "Dominuuuuu vobiscuuuuuu," droned the priest. "ET CUM SPIRITU TUO!" shouted I, twelve years old and St. Joachim's lone surviving altar boy.

At the cemetery a mile north of town, we discovered rainwater standing in the grave; small mudslides were coming loose around its perimeter. Although nobody mentioned it afterward, there must have been others besides me who were secretly horrified to think of lowering Jackie into eight or ten inches of chill water. When the priest finally finished recommending Jackie to God and closed his wet book, I handed him the sprinkler, and he mixed a couple shakes of holy water with the enormous raindrops thumping on the coffin lid. Then I handed him the censer, and as he waved it in the direction of the grave as though it still held fire, a mighty gust of wind swept the cemetery with a fresh squall of horizontal rain, driving most of the mourners back to their cars. The undertaker, with the help of Jackie's brothers and brothers-in-law—no time for decorum now—dropped the coffin into the grave, and that's when it finally struck me—the finality of Jackie's death—when the coffin, hitting bottom, made a splashing noise.

After Jackie's death, I remained St. Joachim's only server for a long time. I suppose it was inevitable that I should become, with my new power mower, St. Joachim's groundskeeper as well.

Every week until I was old enough to drive, I was delivered, with my Toro, to the west end of Main Street and given about three hours to cut and trim the wiry grass around the church and rectory, and every second week I was driven out to the cemetery and dropped off with a lunch for the day-long job of mowing the lush grass around the gravestones. And once a month, from May until October, I knocked on the door of the rectory and asked Father O'Connor for my pay.

Father O'Connor was a tall, pious, elderly man, austere in appearance and habits, who seemed oblivious to the lives being lived around him until they ended. Then I picture him hightailing it through town in his black and gleaming 1936 Oldsmobile, kicking up a cloud of gravel dust on his way to the bedside of some dying parishioner. Typically, an American priest of that era had a housekeeper living in the rectory, but Father O'Connor lived alone. I can testify to the ascetic quality of his diet, for one time he invited me into his spare kitchen— perhaps I was delivering one of his meager orders of groceries—and I found him sitting at his table reading his breviary as he dawdled over a dinner composed of nothing but boiled carrots and icebox cookies.

It always took him a while to answer a knock, for he kept his house hermetically sealed against the summer heat. Dripping sweat on the front step, I would finally see an inner door open and then the front door. "Yes?" said the priest.

I said I'd come for my pay.

"Ah, the grass," he said, and I followed him through the house with no circulation and into his stale-smelling office, where he sat down at his desk, put on his glasses, opened a wide, hardcover checkbook, dipped his pen in an ink bottle, and asked me—I swear to God the same question month after month, year after year: "What's your name?"

Is it strange that I wasn't bothered by this man's detachment? I don't find it odd in the least. After all, hadn't I been brought up to think of religion as a kind of garden the individual entered to find his God, and wasn't one's parish priest merely the faceless mortal who unlocked the door? Holy, to be sure, and smart enough to learn all that Latin, but a mortal like the rest of us and easy to overlook when communion with the Being who created him. And wasn't this the demeanor of all priests? Besides, if your pastor got to know you too well, he could then identify your voice in the confessional, and wouldn't that be embarrassing!

For a long time, I was happily oblivious to the strong current of religious animosity running under the surface of daily life in the village of my youth. How silly we must have looked to the smaller congregations—the Congregationalists, the Methodists, the Church of Christers—we Catholics and Lutherans competing for power on the village council, trying to outvote each other in school board elections, patronizing only those merchants whose theology matched our own, and burying our dead in cemeteries a mile apart. The mind-bending damage must have been done generations before our arrival in town in 1943, for not once did I hear our infirm and inward-looking old priest condemn Luther of Lutheranism, nor did the pastor of Immanuel Lutheran, to the best of my knowledge, disapprove of the friendship I struck up with his son Donald.

Next door to Immanuel Lutheran stood the white frame house occupied by Reverend Schoewe, Mrs. Schoewe, and Donald. Their name was pronounced SHOW-wee, and I was well into high school before I learned how to spell it. They were the first family in town to have television, not that it was always viewable, for the signal had to be pulled in across eighty miles of hill and dale by the antenna atop the church tower. This antenna caused a temporary rift in the congregation, a good many of them scandalized to find their place of worship desecrated by this ugly contraption of aluminum tubing. Fortunately for several of us boys, Reverend Schoewe stood his ground and so, during the fall of 1950, we football-playing friends of Donald Babe, Porky, Gene, Turk, and I were invited each Monday evening to join the family in watching a snowy and scarcely visible yet miraculous rebroadcast of Saturday's Minnesota Gophers football game.

As the only Catholic among these visitors, I alone needed to be introduced. "This is Jon Hassler," said Donald on the first such evening, and his father turned in my direction and grunted, not in disgust or disdain, I think, but in genuine welcome. It was simply Reverend Schoewe's habit to express himself in grunts. He had a very large stomach and a pudgy face. So heavy seemed his expression and especially his lower lip, which protruded in a kind of perpetual pout, that to me he stood for the dour and ponderous weight of Lutheranism, indeed for Protestantism at large, the grave and mysterious error I perceived in all things non-Catholic in those days.

I had met him once before, years earlier, when Donald took me walking on church property, and we came upon his father cleaning trout under the outdoor water faucet at the back of the church. We watched him run his thumbnail along the abdominal cavity of those small, scaleless creatures and flick the guts in the grass, and when he finished and straightened up, Donald said, "This is Jon Hassler," and he turned his very large front in my direction and grunted. I think that day he smiled as well, for it was a lovely warm spring afternoon and he had just returned from the Whitewater River with his creel full of trout.

But it was the school board election of 1949 or 50 that brought the town's religious feuding to my attention. In my novel, *Grand Opening*, it's Brendan's mother who is defeated for the local school board, whereas in actual fact, it was my father, but the method was the same in both cases. After serving two productive terms on the board, my father was drubbed by an uprising of Lutherans who'd apparently decided that four years of service to the community was enough for any papist. A secret phone campaign brought out a surge of eleventh-hour Lutherans whose write-in vote for their surprise candidate amounted to nearly twice the number of my father's supporters.

This experience loosened Plainview's hold on my father, who, until then, blissfully busy in his thriving grocery store, had helped me resist my mother's desire to go back and live among the circle of friends she missed so sorely in the northern town we'd come from. And so, within three days of my high school graduation, Mr. Johnson, a Catholic by marriage, backed his ecumenical truck up to our door, and he and his Lutheran assistant Mr. Brunner went to work loading it with our furniture.

Half a century has gone by since then, and I'm still a Catholic. Holy Mother Church is ailing these days. She suffers from a kind of paralysis that threatens to atrophize her. Her heart shrinks. There's an unattractive hint of paranoia in her eye. But I'm still a Catholic.

She's had spells like this before, of course, some lasting centuries. She'll outlive us all—we have that on the highest authority. What makes this relapse so alarming is the swiftness of its coming on. Scarcely thirty years ago, following Vatican II, she was fresh and frisky, full of promise and optimism. She had the courage to let go of her moribund old language and brains enough to learn a hundred new ones.

I didn't always hold this opinion. Thirty years ago, I was certain the Church had betrayed me, had lost her soul. I fought the changes. Long after she began speaking in the vernacular, for example, I carried my dear old thousand-page missal to church and took comfort in the double columns, Latin and English. If the priest was a rigid reactionary, I paid attention to his homily; if not, I prayed the rosary. But then, a decade after the close of Vatican II, in the process of writing my first novel, I transferred that reactionary part of myself to one of my characters, Agatha McGee by name, and the moment I sent her off to Mass with her rosary and her thousand-page missal, I was free to move ahead with the times.

I have given readings to a number of Protestant audiences lately—mostly Lutheran, this being Minnesota—and I've been infected by the exuberance of their clergy. Young ministers, men and women alike, married and single, speak of their calling with zeal. I sense very little zeal among our aging priest force; they're overworked and weary. Our catholic seminaries are emptying out, and the candidates we do have are not the vigorous men of past generations. "Seminarians" make up two percent of the student body on this campus," I was recently told by a medical doctor at a Catholic college, "and they use up 98 percent of our counselors' time."

Of course, the Church will continue to exist without women and married men at the altar, but what will be the nature of that existence? Haunting me for the past several years has been the vision of a few surviving faithful gathered around one of the last surviving priests, ancient and shaky, saying Mass at a make-shift altar. The setting keeps changing. I used to see the altar hidden in a cave, but that was an image borrowed, I realize now, from the Age of Persecution. I've since found a couple of locations more appropriate to our present Age of Indifference—a storefront church in an abandoned strip mall is one. The other is the priest's cramped and smelly room in an elderly-care home, his roommate across the room moaning in his sleep, the TV at the end of the hallway blaring applause from *The Price is Right*.

I'm still a Catholic because I love the Mass. It punctuates my life like a semicolon; it's a pause, a breather, in my week, my day. I don't pray very well at Mass; in fact, I often don't pay much attention, yet sixty years of churchgoing has left me with a need that's more than mere habit; it's a deep-seated necessity to be lifted up and carried along, time after time, by the familiar words and rubrics. It's like boarding a boat and standing out from the shore of my life for a half hour or so and viewing it through the refreshing air of a calm and scenic harbor.

I'm still a Catholic because I want to be identified with the institution, which, despite her dark ages and her lightweight popes, her blind alleys, her blood lust, her hypocrites in high places, has welcomed people of all classes and nations to its altars; because once, around the time of the last millennium, it preserved our Western civilization from oblivion; because it has left its traces in the cathedrals of Europe, in the scraps of prayers in our memories, in the bridges between continents and generations; and, above all, because it has delivered Jesus's message safely across twenty centuries and is placing it now on the doorstep of the third millennium.

I'm still a Catholic because I believe this message is the most powerful, revolutionary, and sensible cure for human strife and anxiety ever conceived. It's a message so simple that no mere human being could have thought of it, a three-word message so all-encompassing that the Son of God had to come to earth to utter it:

"Love one another."

CHAPTER 4
PHOTOS

In which the reader is invited to browse through the author's family album and pause with him over the faces of his parents and grandparents, particularly the grandfather who qualified as the one genuine "character" in his ancestry, a man needing no adornment when transferred to the novel he starred in.

Here in my family photo album is a studio portrait of a little girl wearing a fancy dress and a flower in her hair. It's a stunning photo, taken in Austin, Minnesota, in 1902 or 1903. I have a framed enlargement of it hanging in my house, and it stops people in their tracks who haven't seen it before. They are struck first by the girl's beauty and then by the intensity and maturity of her expression—she's only two, maybe three-plus something more, a certain tension or apprehension as well as a look of mute supplication. "Oh, Lord, deliver me," she might be saying. It's the earliest photo I have of Ellen Frances Callinan Hassler, my mother.

What could be troubling her at such a tender age? My mother never claimed to be psychic, and yet for ninety years, her phenomenal mental powers—her unflinching observations, her memory, her foresight—were such that I can imagine her looking across the century to the sorrow and depression that seized her during the last years of her life. After my father's death in 1984, the world, for her, became a hostile place. She died in 1991, seven years after she wanted to. Not even I, her only child and lifelong kindred spirit, could comfort her. Indeed, during my weekly visits, she directed this same look of mistrust and fear at me—until a daily dose of Prozac, toward the end, partially restored to me the high-spirited mother I'd loved so dearly as a boy and younger man.

She was born with the century, November 3, 1900, in Austin, a small railroad town in southern Minnesota. She was the eldest of four surviving children of second-generation Irish parents. Her father, Frank Callinan, was a conductor on the Milwaukee Road, her mother, nee Mary Meany, a country schoolteacher. When she was six and her brother John was three, their sister Francis was born, awakening in my mother a fierce maternal impulse. For three years, she cared for the baby as though it were her own, and Francis's death of influenza at the age of three was the first of my mother's traumas.

When she was twelve, her teachers at St. Augustine's Elementary allowed my mother to skip a grade, after which there followed a year of family upheaval, and when the dust cleared, she found herself on the plains of western Canada, where she was set back a grade because of the more rigorous system of Canadian schooling. This upheaval had begun when officials of the Milwaukee Road discovered that her father had been letting his friends ride free of charge between Austin and Minneapolis, and he was fired on the spot. This must have been devastating to a man who loved the railroad as he did, but jolly optimist that he was, he quickly changed course and set off in pursuit of the first of the many dreams that marked the rest of his life—every one of them a pipe dream leading to failure.

Family lore tells me that it was one of his wife's several brothers-in-law who reported to Frank that Weyburn, Saskatchewan, was in need of a laundry. How he knew this is anybody's guess. Without having known the brother-in-law, I picture him simply needing a shirt laundered as he was traveling through Weyburn and finding no one at hand to wash it. And, knowing Frank as I later did, I picture him immediately conceiving of himself as that town's well-loved laundryman—never mind that he'd probably never washed so much as a hankie in his life. Why, he even owned a horse, a family pet; all he needed was a cart, and his would be perhaps the first home-delivery laundry in Canada. And so Frank Callinan set to work moving his family and his horse piecemeal to Saskatchewan.

He and the horse went first, traveling the eight hundred miles by freight train, sharing a boxcar. When he had rented a house, Mary and the children (my mother 13, John 10, Ruth 3) followed by passenger coach. Frank, to ease my mother's disappointment at losing a year of school, bought her heart's desire, a piano.

I have a photo of their white frame, narrow, two-story house standing stiffly at the edge of town, with nothing beyond it but the flat snowy prairie. This must have been where my mother acquired her taste for the unrestricted view, for even though Austin had been surrounded by flat land, at least there was the odd treeline and farmstead to rest your eye on. Here there was nothing but the line of the horizon. Across emptiness like this, you can see a burning house from practically the next province.

My mother, walking home from school one afternoon, saw smoke pouring from the roof of their house. She alerted her family, and they got out, but the house burned to the ground and with it, her piano. This, together with Franks' failure to make a success of the laundry business, sent him on a fact-finding trip back to Minnesota. God knows who told him there was a shortage of butchers—perhaps another brother-in-law—but within weeks of the fire, he was opening a butcher shop in Minneapolis, and his family, larger now with the addition of Edward, born in Weyburn, returned happily to the States.

Graduating from St. Margaret's Academy in 1918, my mother attended the University of Minnesota—tuition in those days consisted of $25 per quarter for a full load of classes—and she supported herself by clerking at Dayton's Department Store. Although she completed her major (ancient history) and her minor (piano performance) and earned her teacher's certificate, her degree was withheld because she did not complete a swimming course required by the university. Fortunately, the burgeoning elementary schools of that era did not require swimmers in their classrooms, and she got a job teaching fifth grade in Lakefield near the Twin Cities.

The following summer, she teamed up with her mother's unmarried younger sister, Aunt Elizabeth, who had also failed the swimming requirement. The two of them returned to campus, cheered each other along the length of the swimming pool, and they both left with their degrees.

This was the beginning of a lifelong attachment between these two women. By the time I was born, ten years later, Aunt Elizabeth had earned her master's degree at Columbia and was supervising elementary teachers in Montgomery County, Maryland, and returning to spend her summers at our house.

(As for swimming, my own inability to swim, indeed my fear of water, comes from an impediment handed down on my mother's side of the family. Tipped into a pool, I sink like a rock.)

Qualified finally to teach high school students, my mother moved to Perham, Minnesota, a town connected to the Twin Cities by 175 miles of the Northern Pacific Railroad, the nation's thoroughfare to the Pacific Northwest. I have photos in my album from the 1920s in Perham. Here is my mother standing soberly among the faculty, and there she is in the distance, on the golf links. And here are three photos from three successive years of the cast and crew of the annual community theatre production. My mother is present in each of these photos looking ecstatically happy, and so is the handsome young man who worked at Kemper's Drug Store, the man she would marry in 1930, my father.

Marriage put an end, after seven years, to my mother's career, for small-town school boards habitually fired women who married. A married woman, after all, took a job away from a bread-winning family man. (Even twenty-five years later, when I began my own high-school teaching career, a vestige of this anti-feminine bias was obvious in the two salary schedules, the women's starting at $3,000 per annum, the men's at $3,200.)

And within three years of their marriage, my mother, with the unwitting help of myself and the Depression, had lost my father's job for him as well. There were in Perham at that time two physicians, Dr. A and Dr. B, as well as two pharmacies. Dr. A's prescriptions, by tradition, were filled only by Kemper Drug. Dr. B's by Mr. Kemper's competitor. After marrying Mr. Kemper's right-hand man, my mother chose to remain with her physician, Dr. B, while having her prescriptions filled by my father, who, with his sixth-grade education and his lifelong adaptability to any situation he found himself in, had become proficient at the mixing of powders, gels, and liquids required of a druggist in those days. In late 1932, Dr. A, becoming aware of this unprecedented crossover, and no doubt urged on by the competing pharmacist, pointed out to Mr. Kemper that the newlyweds were going against policy and either Ellen Hassler, who was now unmistakably with child, must change doctors or Leo must lose his job. My mother refused to change doctors.

Of course, it's awkward for a woman to make such a change in the midst of her pregnancy, but I can imagine my strong-willed mother becoming interested in the moral question as well, defying what she took to be an unfair, and perhaps even illicit, small-town, small-minded policy. And besides, being unemployed, wouldn't her husband finally enroll in the six-month pharmacy school she'd chosen for him in Iowa? The answer was no. Heading south from Perham, they never got as far as Iowa but stopped in Minneapolis, where they spent the winter and spring living with my mother's parents and her nineteen-year-old brother Ed. They were soon joined by my mother's other brother John and his wife Helen, home from New York City, where John had been laid off by the department store where he was learning the shoe business. This was the Depression. I have no idea what they lived on during that time, my grandfather having proved scarcely able to support himself, much less his wife and five lodgers. My father, looking for work in vain, enrolled in a course in baking at Dunwoody Institute—"...to keep from going nuts," he explained; upon his retirement at the age of seventy, he hung his baking-school diploma over the kitchen stove and began baking bread every Saturday for the rest of his life. And how did the seven of them pass the time in that house? "We played a lot of bridge," he said.

My father, for his part, never faulted Mr. Kemper but spoke highly of him all his life. "Business was lagging, and somebody had to go," he said. The following spring, near midnight on March 30, to be exact, along came a major distraction in the person of myself, who bawled night and day with colic.

Six months later, we moved north to Staples, where my father learned the grocery business under the direction of Red Owl's district manager Harry Haney. Ten years later, almost to the day, we would move from Minneapolis to Plainview, the fourth and final point on the compass of my parent's marriage, for eight years after that, in 1951, they would return to Staples, where they chose to live out the rest of their lives.

Here I must speak to Grandfather Callinan. How did I learn, so early in life, that he was the truest of characters? That mother's father, Frank Callinan, was full of bluster, but his gruffness was a facade behind which existed a jolly, gregarious man who loved teasing and being teased? I suppose when I, his oldest grandchild, began calling his bluff at the age of four or five. "Hi, Grampa Grump," I'd shriek, stepping off the train with my mother on one of our frequent visits to Minneapolis. "Why you rascal you," he might reply, and chase me down the platform and sweep me up in his arms. My younger cousins, who never bothered to notice the man behind the mask, spent their visits staying well beyond the circle of his attention, and so my honored position as his favorite, as the Crown Prince of the Callinan cousins, went unchallenged until his death at eighty-eight in 1954.

The year we lived in the city, I was nine, and Grandfather was seventy-seven and reading to me in its tedious entirety *Jo's Boys* by Louisa May Alcott. About the book itself, I remember nothing except the engravings that turned up all too seldom on its pages; what I do remember is how eagerly I crawled into his lap every evening for that lengthy session of drowsy pleasure, my ear pressed against his starched shirtfront and his lulling voice droning on and on, punctuated here and there by the clacking of his store-teeth and by the little whistles and wheezes emanating from his chest after a lifetime of pipe smoking. Coming to the end of a chapter, he'd ask politely, "A few more pages about the boys?" and, of course, I would nod, for despite our difference in literary taste—Captain Marvel was more my style—I was too comfortable to move. Furthermore, there was nothing on television to tempt me away. Television in 1943 was as yet unheard of.

But there were movies. Grandfather and I were equally in love with movies, and here our tastes coincided. Both of us were mightily moved by Dumbo's troubles in the circus, for instance, and we laughed ecstatically at that tree full of hard-bitten, cigar-smoking blackbirds singing, "When I See an Elephant Fly." And I recall the tears of joy and patriotism that sprang into our eyes—as well as the eyes of James Cagney—when President Roosevelt bestowed his blessing on George M. Cohan at the end of *Yankee Doodle Dandy*.

The summer I was eleven and Grandfather was about to turn eighty, we journeyed together by rail to Oshkosh, Wisconsin, for a two-week vacation—from what?—at my Uncle John's lake home. The seats and aisles of the train were packed with soldiers in uniform on their way to Camp McCoy; some even lay sleeping in the overhead luggage racks. All the soldiers within earshot of his voice grew very deferential toward Grandfather as he spun out his skein of railroad stories, pointing out that we were traveling over the very same roadbed he had traveled as a young conductor on the Milwaukee Road. At home, I had stopped listening to these stories, for I'd heard each one about a million times, but now, sitting on my suitcase and witnessing how they impressed the United States Army, I saw them in a fresh light once again. For the first time in a long while, I wasn't embarrassed when pausing to light his pipe, he said to his listeners, "Just a minute now, I have one more story about trains."

Trains were his abiding interest through life. As he grew older, he told train stories with more immediacy, as if they'd just happened, as if he'd just come in off his run from Austin to Minneapolis and back, Austin to Aberdeen—as if he hadn't lost his job on his beloved Milwaukee Road as long ago as 1914.

As a teenager, I was struck by the awkwardness of certain of my friends in the company of adults. The wider the age span, the more difficult it seemed for them to look their elders in the eye and speak in words rather than self-conscious grunts. Entering our house in Plainview, they quite often didn't even acknowledge Grandfather, who, widowed now and spending more and more time as our visitor, was growing deaf, though no less eager for conversation. When they did cast their eyes in his direction, it was only to shoot him an indifferent glance, as though he were an artifact under glass, and I was puzzled by what looked to me like their general hostility toward adults—an attitude I didn't share and couldn't understand. But it probably wasn't hostility at all; it was more likely that uncertainty we feel when confronted with any wildly exotic creature. Yet, to me, no adult was completely unfamiliar because, in the process of bridging the seventy-year gap between Grandfather Callinan and myself, I had somehow learned to bridge the lesser gaps as well.

And how did I get to know this old man so well? By means of stories. The stories he told me and the stories we read together and watched on the screen were a great education to me. His laughter and tears at the movies might have been my textbook on human empathy. And hadn't I delved to the core of the old man when, at nine, I listened to *Jo's Boys* with one ear and kept the other ear pressed to his beating heart? But had television existed back then, how could I have resisted climbing down off his lap to watch *The Simpsons*? (Thus, I've come to think of television as being, besides a crippler of the imagination, a kind of sight- and sound-barrier between generations.) Yet just a minute now, dear reader—I have one more story about Grandfather, in which he amounts to more than merely a sentimental old storyteller.

As an aimless and lonesome freshman in college, I sought his aid in convincing my parents that my best career move might be to drop out and go to work for the Northern Pacific, where a few of my contemporaries were already earning the princely sum of $300 per month. Who better to enlist as my ally than the Old Conductor? Home for a weekend and preparing for bed in the room we shared, I told Grandfather of my railroad aspirations. It took me a while to lay out my motives, and by the time I rested my case, the lights were out, and the only sound from the other bed was the rattle of Grandfather's respiration. Had I talked him to sleep? Or had he, God forbid, turned off his hearing aid before I began? I rolled over and was nearly asleep myself when, up through a fit of phlegmy throat-clearing and across the dark room, came his gravelly voice, "Only a damn fool would quit school to work on the railroad."

I went back to campus, switched my major to English, and spent the rest of my enjoyable time there reading stories.

And here in my album stand my Grandparents Callinan in their Sunday best, posing for a snapshot in their backyard on Aldrich

Avenue South. Grandfather is speaking and scowling, perhaps offering gruff advice to the photographer, while Grandmother, as usual, looks vaguely distracted by worry. Her brother Tom's cancer? Her husband's nephew, the soldier, missing in action? Did her guests get enough to eat? Grandmother Callinan was a serious woman, perhaps a bit less assertive than the typical Irish matriarch, but no less puritanical and loved to the point of adoration by her two daughters, her two sons, and her unserious husband—loved in fact by everyone who knew her and praised by one and all as a homemaker of prodigious skills, particularly in the kitchen, and praised generally for being a saint. And during the year that I, the Crown Prince, lived under her roof in Minneapolis, she, of course, earned my love as well, by simply doting on me and allowing me, on baking day, a thick slice of fresh bread with a sprinkling of sugar on top.

And yet I sometimes wonder: what was truly lovable about her? She didn't exude warmth; she exuded worry. Respect, yes, but love? Unless our opinion of personalities has drastically changed since her day, I can't believe that my grandmother's stiff demeanor of stoic and rigid fretfulness attracted anything but respect. But then, on the other hand, weren't countless generations of us Catholics surrounded in church by cold and stern-looking statues of saints, and weren't we brought up to profess our love for them as well?

She died on a streetcar on her way to Sunday Mass. We'd been in Plainview a year. Our old DeSoto, still running, but erratically, was not to be trusted beyond the village limits. So Doc Kirkpatrick, the veterinarian who lived next door, drove my mother and me the eighteen miles to Wabasha, where I had a "stooper" stomachache in a railroad depot. This was a common affliction of mine as a boy, these stomachaches brought on by stress. They were relieved somewhat by my bending almost double, and my bent-over posture prompted my mother to name them "stoopers." Once we were safely aboard the train to the city, I was fine. We sat halfway down the Mississippi River side of a brightly lit coach with linen towels pinned to the headrests, I on the aisle, my mother next to the dark window, weeping and writing the sad news to her cousins.

At the funeral home, I entered into the exalted presence of my mother's sister Ruth and her two brothers, John and Edward. (These were the names of Grandfather's two brothers as well. Edward, father of the boy missing in action, lived in Fargo. John, a railroader, died young, run over by a train.) Uncle John, a wise-cracking, gregarious fellow like Grandfather, and his wife Helen had come from Oshkosh. Ruth had come from Washington, D.C., Eddie was my favorite uncle. On our trips to the city, he would sometimes devote entire days to my whims and desires—chocolate sundaes and the Crosby-Hope "Road" movies. Later he became an FBI agent and, in my view, the most heroic crime fighter since Captain Marvel.

At the funeral, Uncle John wept openly, and since this was the first time I'd seen a grown man cry, I was embarrassed to look at him. After the funeral, we drove ninety miles straight south to Austin, near the Iowa border, where Grandmother joined her sister Anna in the family plot of eight gravesites bought by Grandfather in 1908.

Grandmother Callinan had been the second of my grandparents to die. Four years earlier, when I was six, my immutable German grandfather, a tinsmith by trade, died in Perham, the town forty miles from Staples, where my father and his six siblings had been born. All my life, I've carried in my mind's eye a picture of Grandfather Hassler as a stern little man sitting stiffly in a straight-backed chair and staring blankly at nothing. He had been mysteriously unwell for many years. I don't remember his ever speaking to me, or to anyone else for that matter. I came home from first grade one day and found our neighbor Mrs. deMars waiting for me with the news that my parents had gone to Perham because my grandfather was dead. She stayed with me until bedtime, and when I awoke in the morning, they were back, neither of them looking particularly grieved. Two or three days later, they went to the funeral without me, sending me off to school instead, and got home before I did in the afternoon. Thus, except for the surprise of finding Mrs. deMars and her aura of garlic in our apartment, Grandfather Hassler's departure from this world—doubtless at my mother's instigation—caused no ripples in my life. I don't recall being either troubled or relieved by his absence when we went to visit my widowed grandmother after his death. He was simply a man who'd existed and now was gone.

Elizabeth Hassler, or Lizzie as my grandmother was known around Perham, was to outlive her husband by nine years. She was a happy, warm, selfless woman of enormous size and many talents. She had helped sustain the family through its many lean years by washing, at the rate of a penny apiece and later a nickel, the bloody sheets and towels from the local hospital. For her services as a midwife, she accepted no payment, nor for laying out the corpse of the neighbors' dearly departed, which she had been called upon to do with terrible frequency during the influenza outbreak of 1918–19.

We visited Perham rather often on Sunday afternoons, and there I played with my seven Hassler cousins, who ranged in age from nine years older to two years younger than I. I found cous-in-play a wonderfully intense form of recreation: being already well acquainted, you wasted no time being shy or reticent; you plunged headlong into play the moment you stepped from the car, and you played as if there were no tomorrow—because of course there wasn't; for tomorrow you were back in your much less exciting home town with all your colorless old friends.

My father, being one of the older children (born 1896), left school at the age of eleven to help support the family. He spent the next decade working at whatever dirty little jobs presented themselves while entertaining higher aspirations. By the time he was twenty-one, for example, he was stuck in the sickening job of rolling cigars for a tobacco enterprise located above a store on Perham's main street, while hankering to follow his two brothers, Leonard and Ray, into the armed services and help defeat the Kaiser. Ray, the youngest brother, was stationed in California. Leonard, fighting in France, hadn't been heard from for a fear-fully long time.

One day in 1918, when people all over town were drop-ping dead of the flu, my father skipped work and caught a ride to Fergus Falls, where a medical examiner slapped him on the bare behind and said, "You're just the sort of specimen we're looking for." This was one of the rare stories he told about his early life—he was ever a man of few words—and when he got to this part, you could see in his eyes, even as an old man, the pleasure he took in that military doctor's encouragement. He had yet to see the military dentist, however, who declared his mouth a disaster. "Come back when you get your teeth fixed," he was told, and so, drawing on his lifetime supply of optimism, he returned to the cigar factory and was saving his two dollars a week for tooth repair when along came the eleventh of November, and with it the Armistice.

I have seen letters written to his brother Ray by my father, inquiring into every last detail of army life—how often did he draw kitchen duty, where did he spend his free time, what kind of guy was his sergeant?—and by his father, who listed the names of everyone who'd asked after Ray's welfare since last he wrote, as well as the names of those Perhamites dead of the flu. Letters to Ray always ended with, "Thank God our family is spared," right up until the day shortly before Christmas 1918, when Otto, 24, my father's eldest brother and closest friend, succumbed to the flu in the morning and was buried in the afternoon—such was the fear of contagion.

Sixty-five years later in 1984, the year of his death, I was reading the newspaper in my parents' living room one evening when my father looked up from his prayer book and said, "The ones who die early are lucky."

An amazing thing to hear from a man who had never been one to complain. Had his life been that hard? "Why's that?" I asked.

"I have prayed for Otto every day since 1918. When I die, who will pray for me?"

CHAPTER 5
LESSONS

*In which the author recounts some astonishing feats of
repression and stoicism performed by himself and his
contemporaries of the Silent Generation and begs his
reader to ignore the injured tone inherent in several of
these episodes—more than one recited to piano ac-
companiment—keeping in mind that the protagonist,
a doted-upon only child, was venturing out into the
cruel world with a skin thinner than most.*

My former schoolmate, Anne, age sixty-two, tells me she used
to believe I enjoyed all those piano lessons that occupied our
Saturday afternoons, hers and mine, throughout our high school
years, which proves how secretive I must have been in those days,
how closely I must have guarded the unhappy episodes of my
youth. But no more so than she, for Anne now admits that she
had no more musical talent than I, and her sense of dread as
Saturday drew near was equal to mine. I find this incredible.
With perfect aplomb, the Anne of my memory rides beside me
in the back seat of the car that one of our parents or Anne's older

brother is driving. Over farm-dotted hill and dale we go, fall, winter, spring, through the village of Elgin, where a couple of my classmates are dating girls said to be beautiful; and through the tinier village of Viola, home of the annual Gopher Count Festival, at which the trapper with the year's biggest collection of gopher feet and tails carries off the grand prize of—who knows?—perhaps a new set of traps, and finally into Rochester and along a street that passes under the shadow of the Mayo Clinic and beyond to the music wing of Lourdes High School. There we sit in the waiting room, paging through holiday magazines and appearing self-possessed despite our weekly appointment with failure.

But weren't you and I, dear reader, weren't all of us, a generation of stoics in those days? Obedient as dogs, weren't we trained by the example of our parents to suffer wrongs and injuries without complaint? While the shortages and rationing of the war made self-denial an immediate necessity, the Catholic sisterhood declared it a prerequisite to eternal life. With this as the first lesson of my formal education, is it any wonder I went through the rest of my schooling as a dispirited underachiever? Next, I see myself safely back in the shadow of the Catholic church, attending Sacred Heart School and learning about God, who seems to me, for all his virtues, inordinately interested in sin. Here, sitting in Sister Simona's first-grade classroom, I'm thinking that maybe school isn't so terrible after all—when tragedy strikes. Out the south wall of windows, I see my mother walking along the sunny street without me. Horrors, she's leaving me behind in this chalky-smelling room with this old sister and all these kids whose mothers, to the best of my knowledge, never take them downtown. I leave my desk and run to the window. Sister intercepts me. My cry of grief must be blood-curdling because she drags me out into the hallway, where I stand shuddering and weeping into the heavy folds of her habit. Her hands on my shoulders are comforting. When I finally gain control of myself, she gives me one of her rare smiles and leads me back to my desk.

"What in the heck was that all about?" whispers Leonard Walkowski behind me.

I don't answer. Leonard is too heartless, too much the mischief-maker to understand mother love. Besides, he's beneath me, for Sister's smile has raised me to a plane far above most of my classmates. I'm one of her favorites.

But Sister Simona had no favorites, a fact I was shocked to discover on the next Monday morning when, after our opening prayer and the Pledge of Allegiance, she declared, for everyone in the room to hear, "Jon Hassler, I don't ever want to see you being naughty at Sunday Mass again."

Naughty? What could she mean? Never in my six years of life had I knowingly been naughty at Mass. All that day, I devoted my meager powers of concentration to reviewing my behavior in church—to no avail. It wasn't until the next Sunday morning, back at Mass with the rest of the first grade under Sister's watchful eye, that I recalled accidentally dropping my Sunday offering envelope on the floor, causing the usher with the collection basket to wait five seconds while I picked it up. Here, then, was a form of naughtiness I hadn't been aware of—causing a hitch in the clockwork precision of the Holy Liturgy. Worse, Sister Benet, our heavy-handed organist, was a true specialist in humiliation. Once a week, at the direction of my parents, I left Sacred Heart School and crossed the grounds to Sacred Heart Convent, a cramped and crooked little house leaning deferentially in the direction of Sacred Heart Church across the street, and there, in a small room festooned with colored prints of the Sacred Heart

and other holy concepts and martyrs, I sat down at the high black piano and played "Here we go, up a row, to a birthday party" and other such trifles for Sister Benet. There were at that time—and I suppose there still are—two sorts of teachers, the punishing and the non-punishing, and by reading the weariness and impatience in Sister Benet's manly and wimple-squeezed old face, I sensed from the first day that she was of the former persuasion. But sensing it did not prepare me for the first slap of the ruler across my knuckles. Subsequently, she proved too bored or tired to bring the ruler down hard enough to cause real pain, but I flinched anyhow, fearing permanent damage to my tender ego.

Having left Sister Benet in that first of my two hometowns, I studied for a time, in Plainview, under Miss Forster in her fifth-grade classroom. This venue was okay as long as I was a fifth-grader, but as a sixth- and seventh-grader, I found it difficult to go back to that lowly room, particularly at 4:00 pm on Fridays when my friends were on their way to the athletic field, and when Miss Forster's late-in-the-week, end-of-the-day breath was nearly sour enough to make me sick.

It should have been clear by this time that I lacked not only the willingness to play; I was entirely without musical talent as well, and yet I stumbled up and down the scale year after year, driven by what?—my parents' pride in me, I guess. By incessant practice, I did succeed in developing one rather lengthy, showy piece each year, and this I would play for company. "Play something for us, Jon," Mother would say, and I would obediently plant myself on our creaky piano stool and pound out the piece of the year, say a simplified version of "The Warsaw Concerto." For the benefit of those visitors who, discovering it to be "classical," would invariably begin chatting long before the piece was over, I would slide into my crowd-pleasing rendition of "12th Street Rag," thus allowing them to applaud with unfeigned enthusiasm while forgetting their pain or boredom at having to sit through the longhair stuff. My reward was the look of pride on the faces of my parents, particularly my mother's, for she was a whiz on the keyboard who'd studied piano performance at the University of Minnesota. The only thing more unbearable than lessons was the prospect of injuring her and my father, and so I plodded on.

Next was Miss Glaswitz, a kindly unmarried woman of fading beauty who kept, with her old father, a neat, over-furnished house on Broadway, in each room of which was a glass-covered dish filled with hard candy. While waiting my turn, I was permitted to help myself as long as I replaced the lid noiselessly. Her father, known as Old Glaswitz, to the disgust of his neighbors, raised a few smelly pigs in his backyard. There was no ruler across the knuckles in the Glaswitz house, no bad breath, no humiliation of any sort, except my discovery that I learned less well under a kindly teacher than a fearsome one.

Was it the unthreatening nature of Miss Glaswitz that somehow allowed me a moment of rebellion, or was it my growing sense of futility? "I can't stand lessons!" I declared at supper one evening. "I never get any better, I never get any faster at reading music, and I never know what a note will sound like before I hit it! I HATE lessons!" I may have caught a flash of sympathy in my father's eye—he'd never been made to take lessons, but he let my mother handle my tantrum because all his life, in all things, he deferred to my mother, and also because artistic involvement of any kind, in that town at that time, was a feminine matter. My mother's reaction was laughter. She seemed so genuinely amused by my explosion that I put a lid on it and went to my lesson.

Miss Glaswitz quit the piano when Old Glaswitz died. He fell dead, it was claimed, in his pigpen and was found with his nose and his ears eaten off. She closed up her house to grieve for a time—not a note of music was heard—and then surprised us all by selling it and marrying a cattle buyer from South St. Paul.

Marcel Proust, I discover, had asthma. He had his first attack at the age of nine while walking along a street in Paris. I had my first attack at eleven. It was a spring evening, chilly, humid. My parents had gone to the store after supper, and I was playing Kick the Can with my friends. I remember the fear I felt as my bronchial tree, branch by branch, began to close off the air to my lungs. I coughed and coughed, trying to raise what I assumed must be phlegm blocking my pipes, but nothing came up, and with each cough, more branches closed off.

"I gotta go," I wheezed with embarrassment to my friends and hurried home just as my mother and father were pulling into the yard. By this time, my breathing was audible: more branches closing off. Mother advised sugar. She spooned sugar into my mouth straight from the bowl, thinking, I suppose, that its grainy texture would sandblast my windpipe. I was getting very little oxygen: more branches closing off. I sat there forcing my chest to expand and contract. What was wrong with me? Though my head had plugged itself up with hay fever every summer, I had been able to breathe without any help from my conscious mind for eleven years, and now suddenly, I was going to die. The sugar didn't work. The whistle of my breathing became ridiculously loud: more branches closing off. In the meantime, Dad had boiled a kettle of water and had me stand over it with a dishtowel draped over my head. Bent over the stove in that tent of steam, I felt the branches open up. Phlegm formed. Perhaps an hour passed before I breathed easy, and when I did, I collapsed into bed, exhausted and aware for the first time of my mortality. This was April 1944.

I was well into high school before I met a truly inspiring teacher. He was perhaps the first man outside my family who qualified as one of my heroes. He taught math and coached football. Jerry Eckstein was his name.

"Come on, Hassler," he called to me one bright, hot, early September day of 1950 during our first scrimmage of the season. "You used to be a better tackler than that!" Having made only a halfhearted effort to bring the opposing runner down, I had twice let him get by me. Well, what the hell, it was hot, and this was merely practice. I was a senior and feeling very important and lazy, the way an old pro in the NFL must feel when he suits up at pre-season camp and watches out of the corner of his eye to see which rookies are awed by his presence. I was a hotshot. But Coach Eckstein cooled me off considerably with that remark. He made me good again, and the Plainview Gophers went on to repeat as Whitewater League champions, and I was at least one-eleventh of the reason.

If being the best team in three rural counties of a Midwestern state seems rather unimportant to you, dear reader, let me assure you there was nothing trivial about it. Our football heroics of 1950 later became the subject of an energetic and rhyming epic poem reviewing the final scores and highlights of the season, from our opening game at Cannon Falls to our heartbreaking, season-ending loss to Lake City, a non-conference foe. Sad to say, this epic, which I composed the following summer in an attempt not to die of tedium during my brief term as an employee of Lakeside Packing, was never written down, and I can't get it back. Of our undefeated conference record, I remember very few details. Plainview 49, St. Charles 0. Ah.

In 1990, having published a novel with a priest at its center, I was often asked if I had once been, if not a priest, at least a seminarian. The answer is no. I had never considered becoming a priest because, as a youth, I was led to believe that I had two impediments to holy orders: I was too unholy and too dumb. These assumptions were instilled by the Catholic sisterhood, who spoke of priests as not only brilliant, but the only specimens of humanity allowed into heaven at the very moment of death. No hanging around purgatory like the rest of us, waiting our turn. Zip—straight from their deathbed into glory. We youngsters envied them this perk, of course, but only until we were told that they earned it by being perfectly holy every day, and wouldn't that be an unbearable burden?

As an adult, while I've met very few priests who were not good, honest men, I've met a number of them no smarter than I, including several of breathtaking ignorance and gracelessness. I recall, in Plainview, a one-day mission for high school students offered at St Joachim's and led by a visiting priest from Rochester. He was a handsome, charismatic young man, and it wasn't hard to imagine myself in his place. He even looked a bit like me, I thought—dark hair, greenish-blue Irish eyes, a strong chin, and pale complexion. Whatever priestly aspirations he might have inspired in me were dissipated as the day wore on, by his unrelenting seriousness. The terrible work of a priest had obviously drained the man of all lightness and humor, and the thing he took most seriously of all was himself. This I discovered at the end of the day when, after having served benediction, snuffed the candles, and spread the altar cloth, I was divesting in the sacristy, and he struck up a conversation with me, asking about my family, my schooling, my plans for after high school. "You're a senior?" he asked.

"Yes," I said.

"Yes, Father," he corrected me. "You address a priest as father."

"Yes, Father," I said.

A few moments later, making for the door, he said, "Goodbye then."

"Goodbye," said I, and because I forgot to say "Father," he turned to me and slapped my face.

It has occurred to me that I may have kept up my unrewarding relationship with the piano, not only for my parents' sake but also because I unconsciously confused it with holiness. Having begun playing under the rough tutelage of Sister Benet and then spending my high school years performing for the Franciscan Sisters of Rochester, I went away to college and spent a year studying piano with a Benedictine monk of St. John's Abbey—a year studying a single piece!

Three days a week, around noon, I entered an airtight practice room in the bowels of the auditorium (it had a soundproof door with a latch like a walk-in cooler), where I would rehearse this difficult nineteenth-century piece, which I gradually came to like (but would have liked a lot better had somebody else been playing it), with its five or six flats, its seven or eight pages of octave-plus stretches of the fingers, and its overall, minor-key inaccessibility. And then once a week, at eleven thirty, I entered into the presence of Father James, a man of cold majesty who lived not with his confreres in the monastery but dwelt among an abundance of pillows and knick-knacks in this extremely un-monklike apartment in the auditorium. Over and over, I played the Piece of the Year, stopping and starting at Father James's direction, nodding my abject agreement at his advice, and speaking to him as little as possible while never looking him straight in the eye.

The relief I felt at the end of each lesson was akin to the ecstatic triumph of stepping out of the confessional shriven on Saturday afternoons in Plainview. Besides escaping the withering stare of Father James, there was the pleasure of entering the refectory, by permission, after grace was said by my seven table companions who had entered in unison, had sat down at a signal and were now about to stand and say grace again and follow their professors out of the room, leaving me to my solitary meal.

The medieval-seeming regimentation of college life in those days, not uncommon on private campuses and soon to be swept away by the sixties, was something I strained against without quite realizing it. Following my instincts as an adult, I have, time and time again, taken the less-traveled road, a habit that had its beginning forty-odd years ago when I sought permission to come late to lunch. How gratifyingly independent I felt, lingering over my meal while the tables were cleared, the floor swept, and the student dishwashers created watery noises in the kitchen. This was 1955. I was twenty-two years old. Finally, I no longer felt like an obedient child.

CHAPTER 6
GROCERIES

In which the author, in tracing his novelistic habits and skills to their beginnings, is led back to his boyhood spent in the Red Owl Store in Plainview, Minnesota, where the episodes in the lives of the shoppers were revealed to him like the chapters of a book.

A very heavy, elderly lady named Mrs. Gitts may have been our first customer. If so, her visit did not result in a sale. I see her waddling along Broadway in an ankle-length dress and turning in at our door, inquiring about the price of something and telling my father she can find it for less at Eggers's across the street. She turned out to be a steady inquirer, not a steady customer, but her visits to our store ended a year or so later when one of our schoolboy employees, a senior in high school named Paul, smarted off to her. "Is this any good?" Mrs. Gitts inquired, examining a jar of grape jam. Paul replied, "If it kills you, we'll give you your money back."

My mother and father, who happened to be standing nearby, heard this remark. My father reprimanded Paul for not showing respect to his elders. My mother, on the other hand, spread the story among her few acquaintances with great delight.

Beyond the occasional drama with customers, there came to be an unforeseen and wider dilemma at the grocery store: closing time. Saturdays were endless. Along the sidewalks, people lingered, discussing their crops and the weather and telling jokes. Some sipped beer in the pool hall while watching card games at the round oak tables or gathered around the pool tables. Some couples went to the show, and too many of these, in my parents' opinion, waited until the second movie let out at eleven o'clock to sell us their eggs and to shop. Thus, the last hour of the week was the most hectic and exhausting, and we dragged ourselves home well after midnight and fell into bed. One night, listening to a conversation from the next bedroom, I heard my father say, "But closing at twelve is what they're used to."

"Oh, they can be trained to shop earlier," was my mother's confident reply.

And soon, my father—surely at her behest—had prevailed upon the Chamber of Commerce to close at ten o'clock.

At the age of ten and eleven, I spent these Saturday evenings doing odd jobs around the store, most of them in the back room—trimming lettuce, bagging cookies, taking the wrapping tissues off oranges—and was visited week after week by a boy named Warren Kruxmann. I think Warren was older than I—certainly, he was bigger—but he was a failed scholar and a year behind me in school. Of course, I was pleased—at least at first. Although wearing an apron like my father's and doing the work I had watched my father do filled me with dread. For I had seen Warren's father around the card tables, paying him no attention, and talking endlessly. Like Warren himself. Having learned from his father that the first thing you did when you went to town was to find a patient ear, and the second thing was to pour your pent-up words into it. Warren, I could see, was well on his way to living a life in imitation of his father.

Like me.

During the wartime manpower shortage, there were a number of women who hired on temporarily and did a man's work at the store—unloading freight, stocking shelves, lugging boxes of groceries out to customers' cars. Perhaps the most capable of these employees, due to her great and muscular size, was Lorraine of Elba, who, after a few weeks, began to show signs of a troubled psyche. I remember the evening she growled at a couple of customers and snapped at my father, who fired her on the spot. She had been brooding for most of the day, going about her work in an absent manner, as though lost in a dream, and now, during the busiest hour of the week, was standing at the checkout counter visiting with an elderly woman she'd known in her youth who'd come in to buy a loaf of bread. They were talking about Elba, a village even smaller than Plainview and hidden in the bluffs along the Mississippi, Lorraine's birthplace.

My father's reprimand—"Make yourself useful, Lorraine"—was answered by a sudden look of fury in her eyes and her voice rising to a screech:

"Oh, don't be such a persnickety old boob!"

"You're fired," he said. "Turn in your apron."

Whereupon Lorraine of Elba dropped the loaf of bread into an oversized bag and told the elderly woman, "I'll help you out to your car with this," and the two of them drifted out the door and down the street, continuing their visit as though Lorraine hadn't just lost her job.

"Here, give her this," said my father, handing me her week's pay from the till. "And get her apron back."

I hurried after them, and when I handed her the money, she looked at it curiously as though she'd already put the Red Owl so far behind her she'd forgotten she ever worked there, and when I asked for her apron, she didn't seem to hear or understand. I didn't insist. I watched them join the crowd at the end of the block, where the high school band was beginning to play, and then I went back to work.

Whenever I read *Fern Hill* and come to the line where Dylan Thomas speaks of himself as "prince of the apple towns," I picture myself going about my father's business on Main Street, and I remember the satisfaction of living in a community small enough to fit your mind around. By the time I graduated from high school and went off to college, I had come to know all our customers by name, where they lived, whom they were related to, and, most important to a novelist-in-waiting, I had watched the events of their lives unfold year after year like chapters in a book: births and deaths, housefires and suicides, new cars and picnics, fiftieth wedding anniversaries attended by hundreds. Although I would put off writing for another twenty years, I've always thought of the Red Owl Grocery Store in Plainview, Minnesota, as my training ground, for it was there that I acquired the latent qualities necessary to the novelist: from my dear German father, endurance, patience, resilience and sound working habits, and from my dear Irish mother, the fun of picking individuals out of a crowd and the joy of finding the precise words to describe them. No one took more nourishment away from that store than I.

Yesterday, having finished writing the foregoing pages, I went for a walk along the river and learned another lesson. Pausing on the riverbank, I considered the leaves hanging orange and golden in the elms and maples across the river and the leaves floating brown and golden on the moving water. The floating leaves, cupped and mostly dry except for that small part of them that served as the keel, seemed eminently seaworthy—destined for New Orleans and beyond, perhaps to some foreign shore touched by the gulf stream. But they weren't seaworthy at all. The leaves I watched float by like sturdy little ships had actually embarked from a tree only thirty yards upstream, and by the time they were thirty yards downstream, some were already flattening out and foundering, sinking the way scenes in books sometimes do when the author presses on with them too long.

The trick, perhaps, in writing as in life, is to move nimbly from one scene to the next, giving your reader the illusion of uninterrupted buoyancy, and not letting him or her witness the demise of style and believability, the lack of freshness, the loss. Walk to the edge of any wooded riverbank in autumn, and, pausing for a closer look, you will notice the countless shipwrecks sinking out of sight. Yet we can be charmed and uplifted by the enduring flotilla that carries on, steadily downstream, confident of new life beyond.

ABOUT THE AUTHOR

Jon Hassler (1933–2008) was raised in small towns in Minnesota. Eventually achieving Regents' Professor Emeritus at St. John's University in Minnesota, he published fifteen novels during his life. The first, *Staggerford*, was chosen Novel of the Year (1977) by the Friends of American Writers, and *Grand Opening* was chosen Best Fiction of 1987 by the Society of Midland Authors. A screen version of *A Green Journey* was produced in 1990 as an NBC Movie of the Week starring Angela Lansbury and Denholm Elliot. In 1996 he was granted an Honorary Doctor of Letters degree by the University of Notre Dame. Having taught English for forty-two years in various Minnesota high schools and colleges, he spent the last years of his life with his wife Gretchen in Minneapolis, where he worked on his memoirs. He died in 2008 after having battled progressive supranuclear palsy for fifteen years.

JON HASSLER: AN AFTERWORD
BY PETER A. DONOHUE

To maintain domestic tranquility, I begrudgingly attended an evening with college teachers. Once there, I found a chair and tried to avoid people, engaging in small talk when approached and otherwise counting the minutes until I could leave.

My attention was drawn to a lone man sitting up against the opposite wall. Slightly older than me, he wore the uniform of an English professor—a sport coat over a sweater and shirt, and rumpled corduroy trousers. What stood out about him was the intensity with which he watched the interaction between the partygoers. His eyes would stay fixed on a person or group engaged in conversation until they concluded their exchange or moved out of view. He would then move on to another scene selecting the loudest person or one whose gestures were the most exaggerated. Little expression crossed his face except for an occasional grin—never a smile—just the slightly raised corner of his lip. He sat alone as if invisible.

Eventually, our host grabbed me by the hand and insisted that I meet the stranger opposite me. She was sure we would be fast friends as he was someone who she knew the world would soon take note of.

The man opposite me was Jon Hassler, an author I had never heard of. He was somewhat awkward rising from his chair, which put me at ease. We politely exchanged introductions as our well-meaning host left us alone—two wallflowers now holding up the same wall. Neither one of us engaged in much conversation, and I felt a bit chagrined at not having read any of his novels.

I sensed that he liked that I was a lawyer and graduate of St. John's. Soon Jon would be in our office engaging us as an agent, attorney and, most importantly, developing a close and lasting friendship.

That initial impression stuck with both Jon and me as the years passed. He remained unassuming and an observer for the rest of his life. Even though he's been dead since 2008, I have many memories that remain vivid and events that seem to have happened yesterday. The publishing of *Days Like Smoke* by Afton Press revived those days gone by and focused me on the unique and delightful experience it was to have been close to a truly gifted man.

We were cautious as we first peddled Jon and his work, not wanting to err or offend. It became clear that Jon was game for risk-taking and audacious positions provided they were fronted by his agents and he could remain "innocent" in the background in the event we went too far.

The slight grin I noticed that first night never changed much and rarely disappeared. Even the onset of what we thought was Parkinson's Disease didn't daunt or diminish the fervor with which he lived and thoroughly enjoyed his life.

That's not to say he was always happy and cheerful. He had his darker moments. When depressed, he would withdraw and most often write feverishly. I remember his publisher once commenting to me—after he married Gretchen—that his writing was so much better when he was depressed. Gretchen was a companion ready to enjoy life, and that they did. His greatest works were on the shelves of bookstores around the world and Jon and Gretchen wintered in Florida or Europe and summered at the cabin on the lake.

Jon purchased the cabin from a fellow teacher with the proceeds from the sale of his townhome to a friend and department head at St. Johns. Jon had bought the townhome with the proceeds from his first major movie deal, the sale of the rights to *The Love Hunter* to Robert Redford. Redford has never found a decent script for the novel, and so it sits shelved.

We learned from our predecessor's experience with Redford and only entered into options to retain the rights to the work if it did not make it to the big screen or TV. This practice proved financially rewarding without losing control of the work.

For me, *Dear James* is the most memorable work Jon wrote. We had developed a close personal and working relationship. I would head out to the cabin on the lake after supper, and we would read the pages he wrote earlier in the day. It was the first time Jon had written a sequel, and he was both reluctant and excited with the idea of an extension of a story previously laid to rest.

He didn't have much choice in the matter. His publisher was insistent on his undertaking the further story of James and Agatha. Agatha was one of his most endearing and popular creations. Having graced the pages of *Staggerford* as Miles Pruit's landlady, she had her own full-length novel as the protagonist of *Green Journey*. Angela Lansbury bought the rights to the story and produced a TV miniseries, playing Agatha herself. Upon its success, she asked for a sequel, and Jon eventually agreed to write it. By the time it was written, the actor who portrayed James had died, and Lansbury could not conceive of going forward without him as her love interest. This just fueled Jon's dislike for Ms. Lansbury as he had envisioned Helen Hayes or Joan Plowright in the role. He refused to watch the movie for years, only relenting when it was hard to find on videotape. He actually liked her performance and softened his opinion of the actress.

Dear James sticks out in my mind in part because one very cold night at the cabin while sitting near the patio door shielded by a lined drape, I could not warm up. Jon admitted that it had been a cold winter in the cabin. I was sure I felt a draft and so began to lift the heavy drape only to find that the patio door was slightly ajar and had been that way since summer. We laughed hard and long at the discovery. Jon never noticed the door and just kept turning up the heat when it got too cold. The man who observed so much of human interaction and relationships could often be totally unaware of the simplest things around him. What a delightful experience it was to spend time with him.

Jon experienced the greatest conflict with his editor during the development of *Dear James*. After submitting the first draft, it was summarily rejected as too short, and his editor was appalled at the condition of his beloved "Agatha." Both the editor and the publisher feared Jon would alienate his readers and cause a revolt at Agatha's brutal fate.

So, Jon dutifully went back to work with a new challenge, this time one he enjoyed. He was intent that his portrayal of Agatha, beat up and broken by the events recounted in *Green Journey*, was the only way to write the novel.

To add length and depth, Jon developed the subplot of Imogine and French as the counterpart to James and Agatha.

One relationship virtuous and the other totally of the flesh. The contrast was brilliant.

Upon submission of the rewrite, Jon's editor wanted him to delete the character French, the goose hunter from *Simon's Night*. He also wanted Agatha's world tidier at the end of the novel. Agatha would never exit a story with so many loose ends. I agreed with his opinion about Agatha but vehemently disagreed with the idea of striking French. After all, Agatha's nemesis, Imogine, had to have French as an accomplice and counterpart to James. Jon won out, the novel was published, and remains my favorite Hassler.

Jon used *Rookery Blues* as a springboard into *The Dean's List*. Having had success in a sequel, he wove his next two books together with the meticulous character Leland Edwards.

We worked closely with Jon on the adaptation of some of his work to the stage. Never a critical success, it did result in a theater named after him in his boyhood hometown, Plainview, Minnesota. Sadly, after his death and with the interest in Jon waning, the theater was renamed.

After Afton Press indicated an interest in publishing Jon's unpublished memoir, I started searching through files and old manuscripts to assist them in its preparation for publication.

Jon admitted during interviews that Agatha McGee was an alter-ego. It was also apparent that Miles was somewhat autobiographical. What was a surprise was the basis for the characters in *Rookery Blues* and *The Dean's List*. We had worked a great deal on the development of *Rookery Blues* for the stage. Certain characters clearly embodied real-life counterparts who played major roles in Jon's life. I had always assumed that Leland Edwards was the bachelor version of Jon. Only upon rereading the memoir and reflecting on Jon's real life did I realize that he was, in fact,

Connor in *Rookery Blues*. As I continued to consider this surprising revelation, I realized that Jon was Leland, Connor, Simon, and there was a part of him in most of his characters, with few exceptions.

I was fortunate to spend a great deal of time with Jon and Gretchen during the last months of Jon's life. He had pneumonia over the holidays and ended up in a nursing home. Gretchen was quick to rescue him and bring him home. From that point on, he had to slurry his liquids because he suffered from pulmonary aspiration.

Jon remained willing to get into mischief right to the end. One morning as we sat in his study, Gretchen brought cookies and coffee. She forgot the slurry powder and so went down to get it. No sooner was she out of the room than Jon looked at me with that slight grin on his face and dipped his cookie in the coffee, ate it, and tried to wash it down with pure liquid. He, of course, started to cough and Gretchen knowing what had happened, scolded him as she climbed the stairs, slurry powder in hand.

Jon left this life the master of his own fate, on his own terms, with great dignity and abundant grace.

Peter Donohue is a third-generation attorney in central Minnesota, where his family has practiced continuously since 1896. He and his law partner, Michael Novak, served as attorneys and agents for Jon Hassler many years prior to his death. They now serve as Trustees of the Jon Hassler Trust.